THE FRUGALNOMICS SURVIVAL GUIDE

How to use your unique value to market better, stand out and sell more

Tom Pisello

THE FRUGALNOMICS SURVIVAL GUIDE

How to use your unique value to market better, stand out and sell more

Tom Pisello

Navigate the Book

Introduction

As a new product manager in a new business unit with a dozen new sales reps, I was tasked with launching a new enterprise storage solution. That's a heck of a lot of "new", and there I was - extremely excited and too fresh to be scared.

I had the naivety of youth on my side, and without thinking twice, set out to meet an all-too-ambitious revenue forecast. My first task was to make the solution easier to sell, so we could get our eager new sales reps up to speed ASAP, despite the solution being saddled with the catchy name "Hierarchical Storage Manager".

How could we get prospects' attention for such a new product? How could we get them to change the way they thought about their current server storage? How could we get them to evaluate a newer, more modern and cost-effective way?

We brainstormed what we thought would be the winning ticket: if we could run a diagnostic that analyzed their current storage utilization and show them how inefficient it was, we'd be golden.

What if we could use the storage profile to show how expensive it was for them to manage storage the "old way" and prove the growth opportunities and management savings of our solution? Bingo.

So, we built a sales tool to turn the sales reps into storage experts – diagnosing issues, quantifying prospects' current costs and making the business case for our solution. Instead of jumping into a PowerPoint product pitch, we trained sales reps to use the ROI sales tool to diagnose the pain and quantify the gain. And they used it well.

We knew we were on to something new – an innovative way to evolve from "speeds and feeds" to a more value-centric approach.

So, we launched a company around the sales tool – my first entrepreneurial endeavor and my first step in what would be a two-decade commitment to developing and refining new value marketing and selling techniques and tools.

In those 20 years, we have made some amazing progress. We've developed sales and marketing tools for over 2,000 campaigns. We've driven ROI business cases for several billion in incremental sales. And we've learned more about the science of purchase decisions– how financial justification by itself is not enough and how to weave modern neuroscience into the art of selling.

And the timing could not have been better. The Great Recession and a "do-more-with-less economy" caused a significant change in buyers and what they expect from B2B vendors. They are turned off by the old approach, and this has caught many sellers and marketers by surprise. This Tectonic shift has rendered many time-honored strategies – like the 4 P's of marketing and relationship selling – less effective.

This book is dedicated as a guidebook that reveals the significant shifts in B2B purchasing. It also provides a roadmap to effectively navigate your content marketing plans and refine your sales approach to not only survive – but thrive – in this new environment.

Tom Pisello

Welcome to the Age of Frugalnomics

B2B buyers have changed.

They no longer rely on sales reps to learn about products or services. Instead, they conduct their own research through Google and social media. By the time B2B buyers speak with a rep, their minds are almost made up. Sirius Decisions reported that **67% of buyers have a clear picture of the solution they want before they engage sales reps.**

Salespeople who try to connect with prospects and close deals are discovering that their time-honored sales techniques are no longer working. They can't just talk about their products and show prospects PowerPoints. They're finding that **today's B2B buyers are Cold as ICE:**

> • **I**n control   • **C**autious   • **E**conomic-focused

In addition to being empowered by online resources, B2B buyers are more skeptical of traditional marketing and product pitches. As a result, marketers are having a harder time getting buyers to respond to their campaigns. SiriusDecisions found that only **13%** of buyers view vendor-created content as credible. And sales reps are impacted as well, with only **17%** advancing beyond the initial presentation and getting a second meeting (Richardson).[1]

Plus, recent economic turbulence has made every dollar matter. **Buyers now demand quantifiable proof that their investment will benefit their bottom line and provide maximum value compared with the alternatives.** This is what we call "Frugalnomics".

Meanwhile, traditional marketing and selling has not evolved fast enough to keep pace with changing buyer demands. **There is a Value Gap between the information that marketing and sales provides versus what prospects actually want to know.**

Here's how some of the most popular B2B sales and marketing techniques are faring in this new market:

Frugalnomics
noun \ˈfrü-gəl ˈnä-miks \
An environment where buyers have become more empowered, skeptical and economic-focused, demanding better communication and quantification of a proposed solution's business value, ROI, payback and competitive advantage.

Value Gap
A mismatch of expectations between buyers, who want solution providers to focus on value they provide, and traditional marketing and selling, which continues to pitch products / services.

81% OF BUYERS EXPECT VENDORS TO PROVIDE FINANCIAL JUSTIFICATION

IDC's research indicates that 95% of buyers require financial justification.

However, two-thirds of buyers don't have the time, knowledge or tools needed to make business value assessments and calculations. This means that if you leave financial justification to the buyer, your sales will be delayed by this shortfall.

Our research has revealed that 81% of buyers expect vendors to proactively provide a business case and quantify the value of proposed solutions. However, only one in five buyers will actually ask vendors for a business case. Instead, they struggle on their own to produce cases or let proposals pile up with the CFO and fail to advance in the approval process.

Vendors that don't proactively provide business cases suffer with stalled deals and longer sales cycles.

Randy Perry
Vice President, Business Value Consulting, IDC

Across the buyer's decision-making journey, white papers are leveraged during the following phases:

Early Discovery:
for finding new ideas and potential solutions — helping answer "Why Change?"

Middle Consideration:
assessing the priority of the issue and creating a short list of vendors, helping answer "Why Now?"

Final Decision:
determining which solution can best deliver the lowest cost, least risk, and best value solution, helping answer "Why Your Solution?"

White Papers: Trade All Your Personal Info for a Sales Pitch

Traditional white papers are likely a staple of your content marketing portfolio ... and for good reason.

According to recent studies from IDG and DemandGen Report, **buyers still rely on white papers when they make B2B purchase decisions.** Your prospects use white papers during all phases of the buying cycle.

However, there's a dirty little secret you may not know: **The effectiveness of white papers has been on the decline for the past several years – with the number of responses and downloads declining 5% last year alone** (DemandGen Report).

To be effective at generating leads and nurturing buying decisions, your white papers need an overhaul for the 21st century. They should take advantage of new technologies and speak to the needs of today's In control, Cautious and Economic-focused buyers.

WHY ISN'T YOUR WHITE PAPER WORKING?

Here are five reasons why your white papers don't have the same impact they once had:

1. Marketing Overload

Researchers have found that the average person receives the equivalent of 174 newspapers every day (MHI Global).[1] This means that people are being bombarded with a constant stream of data on a daily basis.

In addition, SiriusDecisions reported that **buyers now receive 32% more marketing campaigns than they did just five years ago.** Your traditional white paper campaigns likely don't stand out from the pack and are getting lost in a sea of lookalikes.

2. "Download a Call"

Many B2B marketers expect prospects to enter the name of their firstborn just to download a white paper. Then, five minutes later, they get a call from a sales rep. B2B buyers refer to this as "download a call" and know when not to answer their phones.

3. Short Attention Span Theater

The attention span of a typical buyer has dropped from 12 seconds in 2000 to 8 seconds today – that's less than the attention span of a goldfish (Weinreich).[2] According to IDG, buyers think that white papers should be seven pages. However, the average white paper is now more than 10 pages long. White papers have gotten longer to address more complex issues or include messaging for different stakeholders and verticals. However, marketers are trying to convey too much information and are creating boring, text-heavy documents that no one wants to read.

4. Frugalnomics

Today's frugal buyers respond more favorably to content that speaks to their business needs and bottom line. Yet most white papers remain too technical and don't have the value messaging and quantification that today's buyers demand.

5. One Size Does Not Fit All

Due to the Internet and other consumer technologies, B2B buyers now expect content to be tailored to their preferences. However, traditional white papers are one-size-fits-all with little personalization and relevance.

Email: It's You Versus the 'Delete' Button

Using email or LinkedIn InMail can help you connect with prospects earlier in their decision-making process. Although these tools can help you find contact information and quickly reach out to prospects, they alone will not help you break through the clutter.

Did you know that **94% of customers have disengaged with a vendor because they received irrelevant or poorly crafted emails** (CEB)?[3]

Here are five reasons why emails go bad:

1. Snoozefest

You've likely received emails that open with the following:

94% of customers have disengaged with a vendor because they received irrelevant content (CEB)

- "Are you available this week for a meeting?" Your first reaction is probably, "Heck, no! I can't keep up with my current meetings, much less add a new one." Delete.

- "I've sent you four emails and left you a voicemail but I haven't gotten a response." You assume the person is a stalker and put 9-1-1 on your speed dial. Delete (or save for possible evidence).

- "We've just released our latest version of PRODUCT AWESOME and are so excited about improvements in reliability and performance." You think, "I'm glad you're excited about your stuff, but I don't care. I care about my own issues and the 20 other emails I haven't gotten to yet." Delete.

All three of these emails will grab your prospect's attention, but not in a positive way. You only have three seconds to get someone's attention, so your subject line and first sentences count.

2. Information Overload!

How often do you receive lengthy emails from sales reps that tell you everything you want to know – or don't want to know – about their products? B2B buyers have more distractions than ever and don't have time to read long emails. If you want their attention, you must be concise.

3. Too Much Selling, Not Enough Value

Studies have found that 71% of business executives say content from companies turns them off when it seems more like a sales pitch than valuable information. However, 93% of marketers and sellers continue to tie their messaging and content directly to products and services (CEB).[4] Do your emails talk about your prospects' needs and how you can help? Or are they just another sales pitch?

4. One Email to Rule Them All!

If you're lucky, some of your prospects are actively looking for a solution, and your email couldn't have better timing. However, most prospects fall into one of the following categories:

• They're not aware that they have a problem

• They may see a problem but aren't convinced they should change the status quo

• They know that they have a problem but don't know that a viable solution is available and that it can have a substantial positive impact.

Different buyers are at different parts of their journey, so using one type of email for all of your prospecting is not the best approach.

5. "You Want Me to Do What?"

I recently received an email that stood out – but not in a good way – because of how many calls to action it included. Besides a request to schedule an appointment, the email also included three attached white papers and eight links to additional information. Guess how many of these I clicked? More is not always better.

The more your emails try to sell, the less successful they will be. Look at your last few prospecting emails and determine how much you are selling versus helping.

71% of buyers
are turned off by sales
pitch content
(CEB)

93% of content
of content remains
product-centric
(CEB)

From a customer's perspective, PowerPoint decks are:

Not intelligent enough to recommend the right content for the right selling situation. They provide one-size-fits-all content that doesn't speak to the prospect's unique needs

Too linear. This makes it difficult to navigate to what prospects are interested in.

Boring. They lack provocative insights, diagnostic assessments, benchmarks and metrics.

Useless. PowerPoint decks are often short on the quantified financial justification that today's frugal buyers need.

PowerPoint Presentations: Sleeping Pills for Bored Prospects

A prospect responded to your marketing campaign and has decided to spend precious time with one of your sales reps: will this be time well spent or time worthy of regret?

To effectively communicate the value of your solutions, you likely arm your sales reps with PowerPoint presentations. However, your decks are probably doing more harm than good. From a sales perspective, most PowerPoint decks are:

• **Way Too Long.** Sales decks often contain more than 50 slides, which makes it difficult for your reps to know what to present to each unique prospect (not to mention all the time it takes them to weed through and customize the deck).

• **Focused on Your Products.** PowerPoint decks often focus on a company's products and services. They usually lack the content that your sales reps need – challenging, consultative insights that will help build emotional connections with each prospect.

• **Lacking Value.** Presentations often lack the value messaging and quantification that sales reps need to help frugal buyers justify a purchase.

• **Difficult to assess.** You can't track when reps are using PowerPoint and what they are presenting. You also can't collect the customer intelligence gained from each meeting to make your future presentations more effective.

If your customers are like those recently surveyed, then 1/3 of them fall asleep during your presentations. Meanwhile, one in five would rather go to the dentist than sit through your presentation (Zogby).

Your customers are sick of "Death by PowerPoint". They want a conversation, not a sales pitch. They want sales reps to deliver personalized and relevant content. They seek provocative, challenging and compelling insights that will help them achieve a competitive advantage. It's time to reconsider your one-size-fits-all PowerPoint.

Sales and Marketing Not to Blame

Many sales and marketing professionals realize that buyers have changed and are trying to evolve their approach to address this shift. Unfortunately, the driver behind Frugalnomics – a "do-more-with-less" economy – has also impacted sales and marketing internally.

IDC reports that it **now takes 50% more leads to generate the same amount of revenue as it took just two years ago!**

As a result, marketing is forced to run more campaigns than ever, with constrained creative and demand generation budgets. It's tough to innovate when you must do so much without the budget to keep pace.

And it's no better for sales, as CSO Insights reports that **60% of sales time is spent not with customers but on overhead tasks.** The less time sales reps spend with customers, the less they will understand buyer needs. According to MHI Global, **only 40% of sales organizations clearly understand a customer's issues before proposing a solution.**

Meanwhile, organizations are asking sales reps to study more methodology, attend more training sessions, learn about more products and use more content. And they must do this while they manage more accounts, make more calls, send more emails, do more on social media, track more in their CRM and run more demos ...

More is not more.

It takes **50%** more leads
to generate the same revenue
as two years ago (IDC)

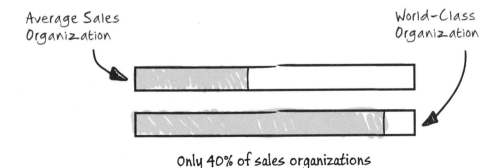

Average Sales Organization

World-Class Organization

Only 40% of sales organizations
report that they clearly understand a customer's issues before proposing a
solution, compared with 89% of World-Class Sales Organizations (MHI Global).[5]

ARE YOUR SALES REPS PREPARED? THE GOOD, THE BAD AND THE UGLY

Each year, Scott Santucci, former analyst with Forrester, asks this question to executive buyers worldwide. The results reflect the good, the bad and the ugly of current sales rep capabilities:

The Good

The Bad

The Ugly

A majority of buyers (62%) indicate that your sales reps are knowledgeable about your company and products. This reflects the time and effort you put into product-focused presentations, collateral and training.

Most reps receive very low grades (30%-40%) on their knowledge of the buyer's industry and preparation for questions they would ask.

Three out of four sales reps are perceived as having little to no knowledge about the buyer's specific business. They also don't relate to the buyer's role, understand the buyer's issues or provide relevant success stories.

ARE VENDOR SALES PEOPLE FREQUENTLY PREPARED FOR YOUR MEETINGS IN THE FOLLOWING WAYS?

Knowledgeable about their company and products
62%

Knowledgeable about my industry
42%

Prepared for the questions I ask
30%

Knowledgeable about my specific business
24%

Can relate to my role and responsibilities
23%

Understands my issues and where they can help
22%

Has relevant examples or case studies to share
21%

Mind the Value Gap

B2B buyers have dramatically and permanently changed as a result of Frugalnomics. They are now:

• **More <u>In</u> Control.** B2B buyers use the Internet and social media to educate them-selves about your solution and the competition. Since they have more control over the sales process, they now wait until their decision-making process is 57% complete before they invite sales reps and channel partners into the conversation (CEB).

• **More <u>C</u>autious.** In a "do-more-with-less" economy, decision makers don't want to make mistakes and are more risk averse than ever. Decision by committee is now the norm, with typical B2B purchase decisions including 43% more stakeholders than they did just three years ago. According to IDC, an average of 10 people are involved in today's typical enterprise purchase decision.

• **More <u>E</u>conomic-focused.** With stakeholders now focused on financial outcomes, 95% require formal financial justification on any significant purchase decision (IDC).

This new breed of buyer is as "Cold as ICE", not caring about when you were founded, how many customers you have, how quickly you're growing or your latest product release. They want to know exactly how you can help them solve their particular chal-lenges and how you will impact their bottom line. Today, it's all about the Benjamins.

95% Require financial justification on any significant purchase decision (IDC)

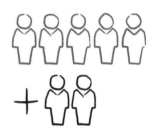

43% more stakeholders per purchase decision (IDC)

In Control   Cautious   Economic-Focused

SIRIUSDECISIONS ON THE NUMBER ONE SALES AND MARKETING CHALLENGE

Interview with Jim Ninivaggi, Service Director, Sales Enablement Strategies, SiriusDecisions

We hear a lot about sales being under more pressure in the coming year. What does SiriusDecision's research indicate as the top business issue for sales?

SiriusDecisions conducts research each year on what is top of mind for sales leaders. For the past four years, sales executives have indicated that their top issue is, "The inability for our sellers to articulate value to buyers". This year, a whopping 71% of respondents cited this as their top issue.

It's surprising to see an issue remain in the top spot for four years in a row. We're not sure why the issue of value articulation isn't getting better. Perhaps the lack of improvement relates to the number two issue – that sales spends too much time on non-selling activities. For example, sales might spend too much time recreating content and not enough time understanding buyer needs and connecting them to the business value of their solution.

The research clearly indicates that these issues are not around sales having enough leads, more training or increased product knowledge. Sales forces struggle to make quota and achieve their growth goals due to a lack of business value articulation.

They aren't spending enough time face to face with customers. When they do meet with customers, they often pitch products instead of talking about business value from the customer's perspective.

What is the Value Gap?

The value articulation issue revolves around improving sales productivity. But it's not just about making more customer calls or spending more time giving presentations. You must improve the conversation by talking about the financial benefits buyers can achieve with your solution.

Our research confirms that there is a Value Gap between the conversations buyers want to have and the ones sales reps are having. Buyers want to talk about their challenges and the value you can deliver- not your specific products.

The issue isn't new, and various training programs and tools have been around a while to help sellers change ... so why no improvement?

Part of the blame is with marketers and sales training. They want sales reps to have more value-centric conversations but instead provide endless amounts of product-focused training. We need to move beyond product knowledge and superiority and focus on what's most important to the buyer.

Unfortunately, we leave it up to prospects to uncover their own challenges and determine what value they can derive from proposed solutions. Instead, we should guide them about any issues they might want to address and the value they can derive from our solutions.

Sales enablement and marketing can do better – providing sales with unique content to fuel a more effective, value-focused engagement.

There is still too much focus on product differenti-ation at a time when products are not too different from one another. The differentiator is no longer the solution's features and price. It instead revolves around the sales experience – the interaction between the customer and the sales rep. It's about how you help customers overcome key business challenges and improve their competitive advantage.

To do this, you can't put a generic value proposition in place and say, "done".

Value articulation must be specific to the individual organization and prospect you are selling into. The sales rep has to understand the customer, their challenges and how the proposed solutions can help them save money, reduce risks, improve productivity and increase revenue opportunities.

The key is going beyond generic to very specific issues and the unique, tangible value you deliver.

TOP ISSUES ACCORDING TO SALES EXECUTIVES:

Rep's ability to connect our offerings to client business issues

71%

Our reps spend too much time on non-selling activities

65%

Inability to manage today's more educated buyer

35%

Lack of useful/relevant content from marketing

32%

Our reps lack the necessary selling skills

29%

Our reps lack the required knowledge

24%

Our offerings do not have competitive differentiation

24%

Lack of quality leads from marketing

21%

58% of buyers
disengaged due to
lack of value
(Qvidian)

Only 1 in 10 sales reps
are perceived as being
focused on value
(Forrester)

In the face of this Tectonic shift, **marketing and sales are now overwhelmed, as they haven't evolved quickly enough to keep pace with the changing buyer:**

• **Marketing** continues to turn up its activity levels, pushing out more product-centric messaging and relying on one-size-fits-all traditional white papers that don't deliver the value messaging and quantification that today's prospects need to spark their decision making.

• **Sales** is also being asked to "do more with less", managing more accounts per sales rep and generating more activity. This means more emails, calls and "death by PowerPoint" presentations that focus on the company, products, features and price – not on the prospect's unique challenges and value potential.

This has led to a **Value Gap** between B2B buyers and sellers. The Value Gap is the divide between a changed buyer and a traditional sales and marketing approach that has not shifted from product pitches to conversations about prospect challenges and the value you can uniquely deliver.

SiriusDecisions found that for the past four years, sales and marketing leaders have indicated that the **number one reason for revenue/quota shortfalls** has not been a lack of qualified leads, social selling skills, product knowledge or sales training – but the **inability for sales and marketing to effectively communicate the value of their solutions to prospects.**

Buyers agree, with a meager **10% reporting that your sales reps and channel partners are value-focused**, as most still pitch products (Forrester).[6] And 58% of buyers have indicated that they have disengaged with a solution provider that has not aligned with their challenges or articulated unique value (Qvidian).[7]

Only **44%** of sales organizations reported
that they are "highly confident" in their sales force's
ability to communicate value messages to customers,
versus 88% of World-Class organizations.
(MHI Global)

SURVIVAL TIPS

1

Recognize that Frugalnomics is in effect, making buyers as cold as ICE (In control, Cautious and Economic-focused).

2

Explore how the Value Gap is impacting your ability to achieve your revenue growth goals.

3

"Break the ICE" by making your white paper and email outreach campaigns more provocative, personalized and value-centric

4

Evolve from "Death by PowerPoint" product pitches to more effective value-centric conversations.

CHAPTER 2

Loss

How a Value Gap Leads to Stalled Deals, Fewer Opportunities and Lost Revenue

This gap between buyer expectations and a traditional sales and marketing approach has a serious impact on your revenue growth. Here are seven ways the Value Gap impacts your business:

1. Trouble generating leads, as prospects don't think they need to address the issues you can help solve. They also don't understand how your solution will provide them with value.

A lack of leads is an even bigger problem in today's market, as it now takes **50% more leads** for you to maintain the same level of revenue as you had two years ago . And it's unlikely you have 50% more marketing budget to make up for this shortfall (IDC). This means you must work harder and smarter just to maintain your current marketing revenue contributions – much less grow.

2. Missed opportunities. B2B buyers are doing more research on their own before they speak with sales reps. SiriusDecisions reported that **67% of your prospects have a "clear picture" of the solution they want BEFORE they reach out to you.**

If you engage prospects earlier and get them to relate your solution to their challenges, you'll have a better chance of closing the deal. According to Forrester, **74% of deals go to companies that engage with prospects early in the sales cycle**, while only 26% of deals go to companies that win the "bake-off".

3. More deals end in "no decision." According to SBI, **58% of a typical sales pipeline end in "no decision."** These are deals that fail to advance to the next stage, because the prospect doesn't have an urgent motivation to change from business-as-usual or doesn't clearly see how the value outweighs any perceived costs or risks. A typical company has a pipeline that's 2-3 times their annual sales revenue, so moving even a small percentage of these stalled deals to "yes" can have a significant impact.

74% of deals go to the vendor that sets the "buying agenda" early in the sales cycle (Forrester)

58% of a typical sales pipeline ends in "no decision" (SBI)

4. Longer sales cycles. Even though sales gets engaged later in the decision-making process, **sales cycles are taking 24% longer than they did** just two years ago (SiriusDecisions). A sales cycle that used to be nine months is now 11 months – causing a two-month delay in revenue recognition.

5. Smaller deal sizes. With deals taking longer, sales reps are often too quick to present discounts in an attempt to close. In addition, procurement is directly involved in more deals and paid on vendor discounts. This makes discounting the rule, not the exception.

According to IDC, **deals are discounted by an average of 20%.** However, I have worked with technology product vendors who discount by as much as 75%. If prospects don't know your value, you'll have difficulty defending your price and will need to resort to discounting.

6. Failure to meet quotas. Accenture found that only **59% of sales reps will achieve their quota this year,** down sharply from 67% last year. If your sales reps don't adjust their sales approach for "cold as ICE" prospects, they'll fail to meet quotas.

7. Long ramp-up times. CSO Insights stated that it **can take over 10 months to bring new sales reps up to speed** so they can make quota. However, Forrester indicated that in high technology and other complex B2B selling spaces, it can take up to three years to ramp up a new sales hire. Even when reps are good at product presentations and demos, they often struggle with business discussions and clearly articulating outcomes. A quick ramp up is where the rubber meets the road, so it's vital for reps to communicate and quantify your value.

8. Wasted selling time. Today's sales reps need messaging, content and tools that show your value. If you don't provide these materials, they may attempt to create their own. However, they'll waste a lot of time customizing presentations and building businesses cases. According to CSO Insights, **over 60% of a sales rep's time is spent on overhead versus with customers.** Each rep wastes up to eight hours a week finding, creating and customizing sales presentations and business case proposals. Plus, after all this effort, they still may not clearly express your value.

24%
Longer Sales Cycles
than two years ago
(SiriusDecisions)

20%
Average deal discount
today (IDC)

How is the Value Gap impacting your organization?

Trouble generating
leads

Missed
opportunities

More deals end in
"no decision"

Longer sales
cycles

Smaller
deal sizes

Failure to
meet quotas

Long ramp-up
times

Wasted selling
time

To find out how much your Value Gap is costing you, use the sales and
marketing effectiveness calculators at www.IWantMyROI.com.

The Bottom Line

These issues can have a huge impact on your sales quota. You'll face stalled deals, longer sales cycles and more discounting. Crunching the numbers for a typical B2B sales team, we've estimated that there are a whopping **$3 million in additional revenue opportunities available for every $1 million in quota.**

To find out how much your Value Gap is costing you, use the sales and marketing effectiveness calculators at www.IWantMyROI.com.

Sales Effectiveness Calculator - http://iwantmyroi.com/#salesEffectiveness-menu

Marketing Calculator – http://iwantmyroi.com/#marketing-menu

SURVIVAL TIPS

1 Recognize that the Value Gap has a real cost to the business, with significant incremental revenue opportunity

2 Visit the I Want My ROI portal and use the Marketing Effectiveness or Selling Effectiveness assessment tools to tally the cost to your own organization

3 Communicate the Value Gap impact to marketing and sales enablement stakeholders to justify investments in value messaging, tools and training

4 Help sales reps and channel partners understand the costs and risks of not addressing the Value Gap

CHAPTER 3

Opportunity

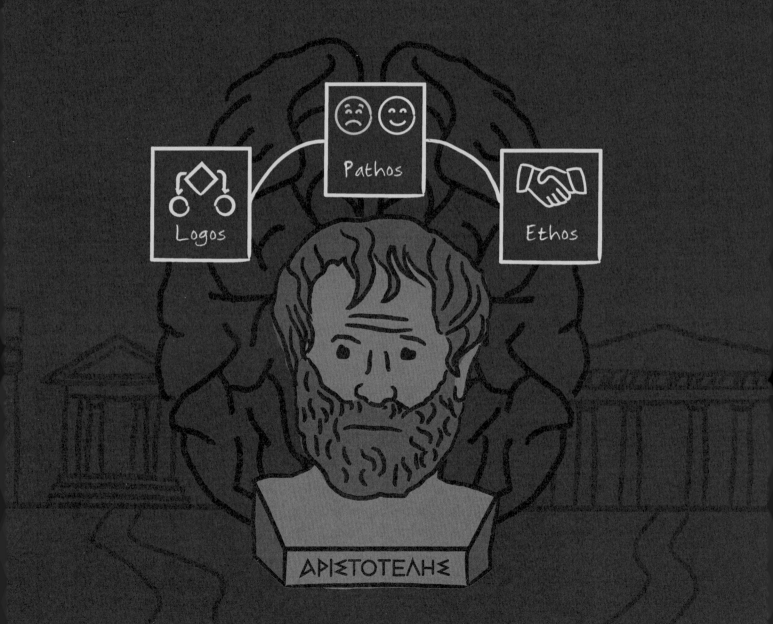

Close the Value Gap to Boost Sales, Order Sizes and Revenue

The key to overcoming the Value Gap is evolving your customer interactions from product pitches to value conversations.

IDC found that when you take the focus off your products and put it on your customer and their outcomes, you can achieve significant benefits. These benefits include generating more high-quality opportunities, igniting the buyer's journey, closing deals faster and increasing deal size – which results in improved sales and marketing effectiveness, along with significantly more revenue.

What Do an Ancient Greek Philosopher and Modern Neuroscience Have in Common? The Secret to Sales and Marketing Effectiveness

In this "do more with less economy", the majority of your prospects are remaining with their legacy solutions – choosing "do nothing" over saying, "yes" to your proposals.

Getting buyers to take action and advance through all the steps of their purchase journey can be difficult. The status quo is hard to overcome, because of bias towards "business as usual".

When asked to change a certain behavior or practice, science tells us that people naturally tend to resist change, even when there appears to be significant benefits in change.

This is not imagined. Research calls this the Status Quo Bias - a cognitive pre-disposition for maintaining the status quo. Business-as-usual is a more comfortable state of mind, because we tend to weigh potential downside risks higher than significant upside rewards. This risk aversion causes a pre-disposed neural resistance to change.

So, how can you break the ICE and get these in control, cautious and economic-focused buyers to overcome their status quo bias and take action?

Status Quo Bias
a cognitive disposition for resisting change and maintaining "business as usual."

Aristotle

Believe it or not, the ancient Greek philosopher Aristotle documented the perfect way to ignite buyers' interest and motivate change. Over 2,300 years ago, he created a guide to crafting winning arguments – highlighting three essential elements you need to make any conversation and proposal more persuasive.

Amazingly, modern neuroscience and theories on how buying decisions are made map the decision centers in the brain directly to these three essential persuasive elements. When you use all three of these elements in tandem, you can light up the "BUY button" in your prospects' brains.

Aristotle taught us that to influence a decision, you needed to **present an argument that contained three critical elements of persuasion.** Leave one of these elements out and you might not achieve the influence you want.

Joining Plato's Academy as an eighteen year-old,

Aristotle was a life-long lover of philosophy and science. Throughout his life, he produced hundreds of books on logic, biology, zoology and physics among other topics.

Thousands of years later, Aristotle's philosophies continue to influence our modern views.

These three elements are:

1. **Logos** – an appeal to logic, the rational behind the decision

2. **Pathos** – an appeal to emotions, a passionate connection to the decision

3. **Ethos** – an appeal of character, to achieve credibility

Enter modern neuroscience and – behold - we find that there are three distinct but interconnected parts of the brain involved in decision making that perfectly align with Aristotle's three elements of persuasion:

1. Logos and the New Brain. The neocortex, in evolutionary terms, is the latest part of the brain to develop. It's responsible for our advanced cognition, including planning, modeling, simulation, creativity, imagination, awareness and language. This is the thinking part of our brains and is responsible for logic. Our advanced neocortex makes us uniquely human.

2. Pathos and the Reptilian Brain. On the other end of the spectrum, this is the oldest part of the brain is and is thought to have evolved over 400 million years ago. This part of the brain is responsible for survival, subconsciously processing our environment and reacting to keep us alive. Think of a reptile, how territorial they are and how quickly they react to danger. This part of the brain is also responsible for emotion.

3. Ethos and the Middle Brain. Often referred to as the "limbic brain", this part of the brain is associated with social and nurturing behaviors, mutual reciprocity and trust. In evolutionary terms, the Middle Brain arose during the age of the mammals and is connected to our digestive system. It's responsible for the "gut feel" we get when making decisions. This part of the brain is also responsible for measuring credibility, so important in decision-making.

Each of these buying centers in the brain aligns with an element of Aristotle's art of persuasion. Because the buying centers are connected, you need all three to persuade buyers to move from "do nothing" to "yes."

Paul D. MacLean, an American Neuroscientist, proposed the theory that the human brain is actually constructed from three distinct but interconnected brains. This is known as the Triune Brain theory. MacLean expanded on this theory in his 1990 book "The Triune Brain in Evolution."

Logos

Pathos

Ethos

Logos: Appeal to Logic and Reason

Neo-Cortex

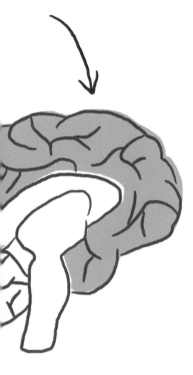

Logos is associated with the neo-cortex. The neo-cortex is also known as the New Brain, as it was the latest part of the brain to evolve. This is the "thinking" part of our brain and is responsible for our logic.

To stimulate a prospect's neo-cortex, you must help them rationalize and justify their purchase. But how do you convince someone logically that your solution is the best?

You must provide them with rational and financial justification to close the Value Gap. To do this, you can use the following key elements:

Value Map

The first step to appeal to a prospect's Logos is documenting your value and clearly articulating it to prospects. I recommend grouping "value" into one of four categories as shown in the Value Map chart.

The X-axis moves from tactical to strategic, while the Y-axis moves from tangible benefits to intangible / soft benefits that are harder to quantify.

Point of Value

The second step to appeal to a prospect's Logos is recognizing that value is not the same for all of the buyers who are involved in a purchase decision. Each buyer has a unique perspective on value including which challenges and business benefits matter the most.

Generic doesn't cut it.

43% of enterprises involve at least 10 people in a purchase decision. This means you must quantify your value for each stakeholder. (IDC)

Buyers care about their goals, challenges and aspirations. For example, the supply chain manager cares about inventory turns, carry costs and scrap. The business unit cares about time to market and quality. The technical team cares about TCO and security. All of these prospects work for the same organization and are evaluating the same solution, but they have wildly different opinions on what makes it valuable.

Intangible

Risk Avoidance

Help your prospect identify and mitigate business risks. This includes avoiding losses from regulatory issues, fraud, theft, security breaches, disasters and downtime.

Revenue Growth

Identify and capture lost revenue opportunities. You can also create new sales and market opportunities – through faster time to market, new products, new territories, etc.

Tactical

Strategic

Cost Savings

Recognize your buyer's cost challenges and help them reduce their current capital or operating expenses. This can include reducing their travel or telecommunications costs, as well as avoiding the purchase of new IT equipment to replace something that's obsolete.

Productivity or process improvements

Identify inefficiencies to help your prospect reduce labor costs and boost productivity. This can include reducing the time, resources or skill level needed to complete tasks. It also includes streamlining processes to reduce errors and eliminate waste.

Tangible

VALUE MAP IN ACTION

A financial management and reporting provider wanted to better articulate the benefits that they provide CFOs and other prospects.

Most of their prospects have an on-premise, centralized reporting system. They rely mostly on spreadsheets to collect budgets and forecasts from different parts of the organization.

Using the Value Map framework – starting with the most tactical and tangible to the more strategic and intangible – the provider is able to discuss the challenges they address and benefits they provide.

This framework helps the team think differently about their value, uncover benefits and solve buyer challenges.

Here's the business value the team uncovered:

Risk Avoidance

- Reduce risk due to planning errors
- Reduce compliance and regulatory reporting risks

Revenue Growth

- Improve forecast accuracy to better identify and capture new business opportunities
- Better handle business change, having more confidence in the actuals and the future when the business changes

Cost Savings

- Reduce the costs of financial management and reporting
- Eliminate expensive maintenance agreements for legacy solutions
- Reduce IT's costs for on-premise support and hosting the legacy system
- Align the budget with where money needs to be spent and drive down costs

Productivity or process improvements

- Reduce the time and effort spent identifying data issues and inconsistencies
- Reduce the time and resources spent on spreadsheets, along with configuring hard-to-use budgeting and planning solutions
- Spend less time collecting data and crunching numbers and more time on analysis

TANGIBLE VS INTANGIBLE

The Value Map can get your team thinking beyond the basic buyer challenges and your solution's benefits, to consider the less tangible benefits (which are often the most important to motivate purchase decisions).

The Tangible Benefits like Cost Savings and Productivity / Process Improvements are often easy to quantify, and are relatively solid. When you quantify a Tangible Benefit, you can typically measure the impact and realize the benefit. For example, let's say a customer implements your solution and as a result, they can retire a legacy solution and avoid annual support and maintenance contract costs, and avoid an expected upgrade in a year. There is a direct link between implementing the solution and deriving these concrete benefits.

Less tangible benefits such as Risk Avoidance and Revenue Growth are often harder to quantify and more difficult to realize, but tend to have a bigger emotional influence in driving purchase decisions. Even though they are harder to visualize and quantify, they can be more important to include in your value messaging and benefits tally.

Intangible benefits are by definition more abstract and less concrete. The less tangible benefits typically require multiple "success steps" in order to realize the benefits.

For example, to realize Revenue Growth from a proposed sales effectiveness solution, the solution has to be deployed, the sales rep needs to adopt it, and then use the solution a certain way, having it influence an often fickle and frugal prospect. That's a lot of "success steps" with much uncertainty to gain the benefit – less concrete and reliable, but if realized, often more significant to the business compared to the proposed solution's tangible benefits.

Intangible

adjective \in'tanjəb(ə)l\

unable to be touched or grasped; not having
physical presence.

Value Map Calculation Examples

Here are a couple of simple examples of how to use the Value Map categories to not just classify, but quantify the current costs and benefits:

Cost Savings Example

A typical example of a cost savings calculation: Migrating from on-premise servers to a cloud infrastructure as a service (IaaS) solution.

Current Cost (As Is)

Current number of servers	10
Avg. annual cost per server (support contracts, power, cooling, space)	$5,000
Avg. annual server operating costs	$50,000

Proposed (To Be)

Current number of servers	10
Avg. cost per server per month	$250
Avg. annual server operating costs	$30,000

Productivity Improvement Example

A typical example of a productivity improvement savings calculation: A solution to help reduce the time sales reps searching for or recreating / customizing content they need for customer engagements.

Searching for / Recreating Content	Current (As Is)	Benefits with Proposed Solution	Proposed (To Be)
Person hours per week sales reps spend trying to find / recreate content	5.0	20%	4.0
Work weeks per year	48		48
Average burdened labor rate (per hour)	$45.00		$45.00
Total annual costs per sales rep	$10,800	$2,160	$8,640
Total number of sales reps	100		100
Total annual costs per year	$1,080,000	$216,000	$864,000

Risk Avoidance Example

A typical example of a risk avoidance calculation: A proposed solution can help reduce the chance of a security breach, as well as limit the scope when a breach occurs.

Security Risks	Current (As Is)	Benefits with Proposed Solution	Proposed (To Be)
Risk of a security breach over next 12 months	20%	33%	13%
Average cost of a security breach	$3,200,000	20%	$2,560,000
Total annual security risk	$640,000	$307,200	$332,800

Revenue Growth Example

A typical example of a revenue growth calculation: A proposed solution can help reduce the time it takes for sales reps to ramp up, helping accelerate time to effectiveness.

Sales Rep Ramp Up	Current (As Is)	Benefits with Proposed Solution	Proposed (To Be)
Number of new sales reps	10		10
Average quota per rep	$2,000,000		$2,000,000
Quota performance during ramp up	50%		50%
Average ramp up time (in months)	10.0	33%	6.7
Lost revenue during ramp up per rep	$833,333	$275,000	$558,333
Total lost revenue	$8,333,333	$2,750,000	$5,583,333

Challenges

Pain Points

Cost of
"Do Nothing"

Your
Unique
Value

Benefits
of Change

Key
Improvements

Solutions /
Features

Challenge-Centric Approach

The third step to appealing to Logos is communicating your value from the buyer's perspective – not yours. B2B organizations often communicate from an inside-out perspective. They say, "Here's our solution and the benefits it can provide." When they give sales presentations, they spend the first 10 minutes providing a company overview.

When B2B organizations differentiate their solutions, they often talk about each feature they perceive as a differentiator. However, buyers don't care about your company or why your solution is superior. They begin their journey – not with your solutions – but with their business challenges.

If you want to move buyers from doing nothing to saying, "yes," you must **start conversations by talking about your prospects' pains.** Identify and diagnose their challenges. Show prospects how much these challenges are costing them. Then – once they see the problem and costs – align their challenges with your solution. State the specific benefits that you can provide.

A challenge-centric approach promotes collaboration with buyers and focuses on:

1. The **buyer's challenges** aligned to each decision maker you engage with, because each role has different key issues.

2. The **pain points** these challenges cause each decision maker. Identify the key performance indicators (KPIs) affected and how these compare to peer benchmarks. These KPIs include ROI, net present value savings, payback period and internal rate of return. For more information about these indicators, see the Appendix.

3. The **cost of doing nothing.** Quantify how the challenge has led to overspending, productivity losses, process inefficiencies, business risk and revenue shortfalls.

4. **Facilitating the buyer's journey** and provide them with the right message at the right stage in their decision-making process.

These challenges aren't random but focused on those issues your solution can best address. **This will move the conversation towards your ultimate goal – a sale.**

WHAT A SOLUTION-FOCUSED VERSUS A CHALLENGE-FOCUSED APPROACH LOOKS LIKE

Too often, organizations try to quantify their value by talking about their solutions first – not the customer's challenges first.

"Solution first" means determining how the solution and its features drive savings. It's about what the solution can do for the buyer.

"Challenge first" doesn't mean abandoning the solution. It discusses the buyer's challenges first and then how the solution can address them.

It's a subtle but important shift in perspective that will dramatically improve the effectiveness of your value conversations. Let's look at examples of a solution-focused and challenge-focused approach:

Solution-focused approach

• Our medical imaging solution has several features that make it easier to set up a patient to be imaged.

• This can help your technicians reduce their repositioning, post-patient processing and handling times.

• Because of these features, each image takes five minutes less. With three images for the average patient, each technician can save at least 15 minutes per patient.

• This means you can schedule an additional patient each hour, potentially eight more per day.

• Here's the overtime costs you can save and additional revenue you can generate …

Challenge-focused approach

• Most imaging centers I visit are experiencing challenges that I think you can relate to.

• Did you know that …

  • 23% of imaging centers are extending their business days by two to three hours just to handle current patient demand.

  • Imaging centers are experiencing 30% year-over-year margin impact to meet the growing demand.

  • 50% more patients are available if imaging centers could improve their efficiency.

• I understand that you may be experiencing similar issues, keeping the imaging center open after hours to handle current patient workloads. You are paying your technicians overtime, which makes these extended hours less efficient. You also likely could see more patients but you currently don't have the room or staff for additional imaging. Is this correct?

• What if you could, within your existing facilities and with your current technicians, see an additional patient each hour? What could this mean to your business in terms of capturing additional patient demand while reducing operating costs and maintaining margins?

• Our medical imaging solution can help you with …

• Let me calculate what these benefits could mean to you …

Decision science points out
that buyers are more motivated to move away from pain, than to maximize their gains. Especially early in the sales process, seek to "quantify the pain" of sticking with the status quo before "justifying the gain" from your proposed solution.

Different Value for Each Stage of the Journey

The fourth step to appealing to a buyer's Logos is communicating different values, depending on where he or she is in the decision process. Depending on the stage in the sales cycle, your prospect may:

• Not believe they have the issue you want to address

• Know they have the issue but it's not high on their priority list

• Not have buy-in from other stakeholders

• Not have the time, or the resources, or the budget to commit to the proposal

• Perceive the proposal as too risky

• Think a competitor offers better value than you

How can you overcome these objections to help buyers make a decision?

For each stage, you must communicate and quantify your value. Here's how:

• Ideas Stage. Early in the decision-making process, buyers may not be aware of the important challenges they need to address. If they are aware, they may not prioritize their key issues.

During this stage, don't talk about why your product is amazing. After all, buyers may not even realize they have an issue, let alone that they should buy your product to fix it.

Instead, illuminate the buyer's challenges, so they see these issues as a top priority. At this early stage, it's important to help buyers identify and diagnose issues, just like a doctor would. Then, you should **quantify the pain.** Tally the cost of doing nothing to show buyers what maintaining the status quo is costing them.

• Exploration and Evaluation Stages. In the middle stages of the buyer's journey, prospects are starting the search for solutions. You should answer the question, "Why now?" Prospects need to overcome serious doubts. They want validation that your solution can solve their issue and deliver tangible business benefits at low risk.

It's important to **justify the gain,** proving that you can solve the buyer's top challenges. Discuss how you can help buyers reduce costs, improve productivity, streamline processes, mitigate risks and drive incremental revenue. At this stage, buyers want to know that you can deliver significant and quick ROI.

Credibility also matters during this phase. You must provide evidence – via success stories – that the buyer's peers have achieved these gains.

• **Selection Stage.** In this final stage, the prospect is comparing and contrasting vendors. The big question to answer is, "Why you?"

At this stage, you must **prove you are not the same.** Quantify that you have a lower TCO and will deliver big benefits with minimal risk.

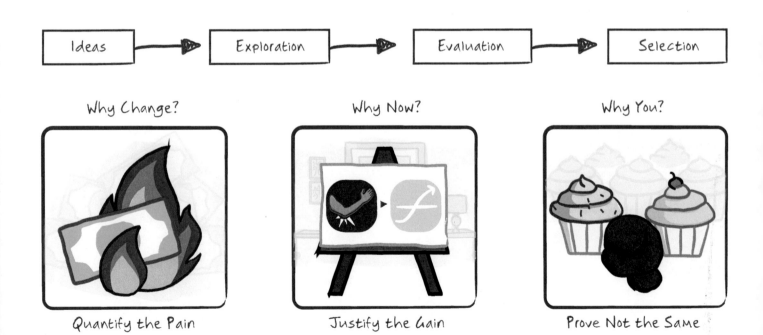

HOW TO SHOW KEY DECISION MAKERS YOUR VALUE

More stakeholders than ever are now involved in key purchase decisions. This means you aren't selling to just one person but to at least five different decision makers. According to IDC, purchases over $500,000 have at least 10 decision makers. Each of these decision makers has their own ideas about which challenges are the most important, what your solution should do to address these challenges and the business value they want to derive.

Value is truly in the eye of the beholder. Along with a "point of view", each stakeholder has a unique "point of value". You must align your value with each stakeholder's top challenges.

Let's look at a web conferencing solution and see how different stakeholders have different points of value:

Sales

The sales team is challenged to provide a better customer buying experience. They must maximize their effectiveness and increase the amount of time that reps spend with customers, while reducing travel costs.

The value is replacing a legacy solution that wasn't effective for sales. Instead of spending much of a conference call getting people into the meeting, reps can now spend more time talking to prospects. The solution improves the reps' ability to share high-quality videos and do demos, all while reducing travel costs.

Training

Training is challenged to provide more effective educational content and services to its expanding global workforce. The training team also needs to bring new sales hires up to speed quickly.

The value is replacing a legacy solution that doesn't have the video features the training team needs to collaborate with trainees and share educational materials.

Marketing

Marketing's challenge is easily delivering large-scale, live and on-demand webcasts. Marketing also wants to deliver these webcasts more frequently and with higher quality.

The new solution makes it easier to set up and manage large, live webcasts. It provides high-quality video, polling, screen sharing, demos, whiteboards and annotation. Recordings are high quality with enhanced tracking, so marketing can see how different prospects interacted with the on-demand content.

IT

The challenge is providing a web conferencing solution that has a low cost of ownership and doesn't burden IT.

The value is replacing the legacy solution with one that is easier for each region to configure and manage on its own – meaning fewer calls to support. Since the new solution is cloud-based, it also reduces infrastructure, maintenance and licensing costs.

HR

HR's challenge is finding a web conferencing solution that supports the business' expanding worldwide operations. HR wants to source team members from anywhere in the world and support a mobile workforce.

The value is replacing a legacy solution that isn't easy to use on a global scale and doesn't support mobility. The new video conferencing tools improve hiring speed and effectiveness by allowing managers to "see" candidates ahead of time versus just speaking with them on the phone.

Justifying an Investment: By the Numbers

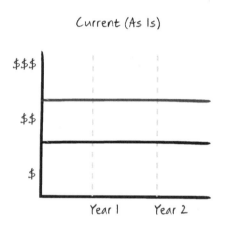

Current (As Is)

$$$

$$

$

Year 1   Year 2

● Revenue   ● Expenses

To calculate and communicate value, one of the most common methods to apply is a cash flow analysis, comparing the costs and benefits over time. This is more commonly referred to as an ROI analysis.

The analysis is used to measure the value of a proposed project over a pre-established time frame, usually set up to match the useful life of the solution (typically 3 to 5 years). The analysis compares the cost savings and business benefits of a proposed solution versus the total investments and costs in order to determine whether the project makes logical sense. Because of this, ROI analysis is often referred to as "making the case for change", providing the analysis and proof points as to whether the proposed project / change makes fiscal sense.

A typical ROI analysis compares the "business as usual" financials, where the organization continues to operate as it intends to without the solution (often called As Is), with a predictive model of the financial scenario where the solution is implemented (often called To Be).

For technology solutions and services, the analysis is usually performed over 3 to 5 years to match the proposed lifetime of the investment or service contract term, but this time period can be longer for solutions that have longer useful lives (like manufacturing / industrial equipment) or lengthier business service contracts.

The financial model considers the revenue and expenses for the business over time.

The business revenue and expenses in the As Is (before) scenario are compared with the revenue and expenses of the predicted To Be (after) scenario to determine the impact of the solution, and the overall cash flow of the project.

To calculate the value of the proposed solution, the analysis first starts with an understanding of revenue and expense projections for the current business (before the solution) over the analysis period. The team gathers current revenue and expenses, and projections of how the revenue and expenses are expected to grow without implementing the proposed solution. This is the "As Is" state and provides a clear understanding for the buyer as to the current "cost of do nothing", critical in getting the buying committee motivated on making a change and making it a priority.

Cost of Do Nothing

A tally of the current costs, lost productivity, process issues, risks and lost revenue opportunities related to legacy systems and practices.

In some cases, if the project only focuses on impacting business savings and revenue is not relevant, the revenue portion of the analysis may be excluded, however, revenue growth is becoming a critical goal of more projects and should be included where it is relevant.

Next, the impact of your proposed solution is simulated and the impact projected against the As Is revenue / cost projections to determine:

• What incremental investment is required?

• What are the business benefits: the cost reductions, productivity / process improvements and risk mitigation against the expenses and risk mitigation / revenue growth against the As Is Revenue?

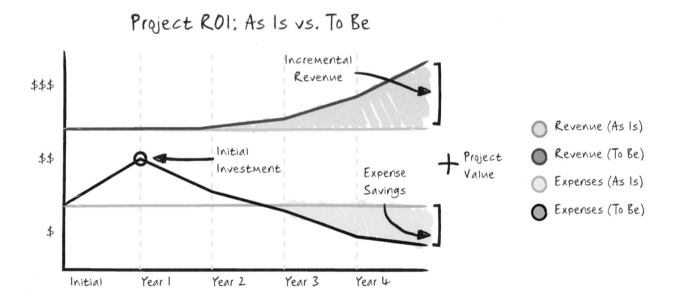

The simulation first lets the business tally the level and duration of required solution investments.

Most projects require some kind of up-front investment. For proposals including a purchase of equipment or software, the purchase price of the equipment is often up-front. For over-time service contracts, the up-front expenses include planning, integration, training and roll-out labor. Almost all projects have some kind of up-front costs, and these are tallied at time "Initial" / zero.

Over time, the expenses include service contract costs, support contracts, management, supplies, and evolution costs. It is important to tally not just the upfront expenses, but to understand and estimate the on-going total costs of the proposed investment.

The financial simulation of the proposed solution also predicts the magnitude of benefits, tallying the cost savings, productivity / process improvements, risk mitigation and revenue impacts, and importantly, how quickly the benefits can be realized.

Example As Is vs. To Be Comparison

	Initial	Year 1	Year 2	Year 3
Revenue				
As Is	$100,000,000	$110,000,000	$121,000,000	$133,100,000
To Be	$100,000,000	$110,100,000	$133,100,000	$159,720,000
Net Revenue Impact	$0	$1,100,000	$12,100,000	$26,620,000
Net Margin Impact (20%)		$220,000	$2,420,000	$5,324,000
Expenses				
As Is	$20,000,000	$220,000,000	$24,200,000	$26,620,000
To Be	$20,220,000	$21,950,000	$24,600,000	$27,370,000
Net Expense Savings	$220,000	$50,000	$400,000	$750,000
Total Benefits	$220,000	$270,000	$2,020,000	$4,574,000

In modeling the benefits, it is important to factor that the benefits are not realized right away. First, there is a deployment period that should be accounted for. In the beginning of the proposed project, investments will occur (like equipment purchases, planning and development) well before the proposed solution is deployed. Benefits are therefore delayed until after the proposed project gets rolled out.

Once deployed, the solution won't immediately start yielding all expected benefits. Many of the predicted benefits require adoption, training and process improvements in order to begin netting expected revenue growth or savings, and this can take months to realize the full benefits. Often a "realization curve" is applied to better predict the real returns.

Once the investments and benefits of the proposed solution are quantified, the incremental costs versus the benefits are compared. The difference between the Expenses and Revenue (factored to include only the net margin impact) for the As Is and To Be are tallied, to create a "cash flow" over time.

When the difference is calculated, if the To Be is more costly that the As Is, at least for that time period, the project doesn't make fiscal sense. This can be the result of a high investment requirement, with a long time to accumulate benefits. Over time, the predicted benefits should to overcome the initial and over-time investments to yield positive cash flow.

Cash Flow Analysis
a tally of the predicted benefits versus proposed investments in the solution.

Discounted Cash Flow Analysis
a cash flow analysis where the time value of money is factored into the analysis.

According to Investopedia, "the time value of money is "the idea that money available at the present time is worth more than the same amount in the future due to its potential earning capacity. This core principle of finance holds that, provided money can earn interest, any amount of money is worth more the sooner it is received."

A discounted cash flow analysis rightfully factors that projects which require up-front investments need to tally that each dollar spent today on the proposal is a little more valuable than each dollar of future benefit received.

Example Cash Flow Analysis

	Initial	Year 1	Year 2	Year 3
Solution Investment	$220,000	$100,000	$100,000	$100,000
Benefits		$270,000	$2,020,000	$4,574,000
Net Benefits (Benefits - Investments)	$220,000	$170,000	$1,920,000	$4,474,000
Cumulative Benefits	$220,000	$50,000	$1,870,000	$6,344,000

As financiers like to net out results, several key financial formulas are used as indicators, derived from the cash flow analysis results. These typically include:

• **Return on Investment (ROI)** – a ratio of the net benefits divided by the total investment. A higher ratio means that the projects net benefits are much higher than the investment, and the project is often judged as less risky as a result. To calculate the value, ROI = net benefits / total investment, where net benefits are equal to total benefits – total investment.

• **Net Present Value (NPV) Savings** – a calculation that measures the net benefit of a project in today's dollar terms using a discount rate to discount future cash flows. Many times a project requires up-front investment, and this is more expensive in time value of money terms compared to future benefits, so looking at the cash flows over time assures that all cash flows over time are made equivalent. Sometimes a project may have a positive cash flow, but because of a large upfront investment and a long time to accumulate benefits, may actually have a negative NPV savings. A high NPV savings indicates that the project can deliver real bottom-line impact to the organization.

• **Payback Period**- The payback period is the time frame needed for the project to yield a positive cumulative cash flow, which is typically specified in months. The payback period starts by comparing cumulative costs versus cumulative benefits by month from the beginning of a project until the point when the cumulative benefits exceed the cumulative costs. A quick payback on a project usually is a sign of less risk.

• **Internal Rate of Return (IRR)** – The IRR calculates the effective interest rate that the project generates. A higher interest rate than competitive projects means that the project has a higher return and generates more effective interest on the investment. In mathematical terms, the Internal Rate of Return is calculated as the projected discount rate that makes the Net Present Value calculation equal to zero. The method of calculation involves a series of guesses, making it the most difficult to understand, but when comparing projects, one of the most effective metrics in selecting the best comparative project.

• **Total Cost of Ownership (TCO)** - A tally of not just the purchase cost of a product or service, but all of a solution's costs over its lifecycle. This includes the upfront costs to plan, customize, integrate and deploy the solution; running costs including support, management, facilities and maintenance; and the retirement costs at the end of the solution's life. For assets such as computing systems, the purchase price is less than one-third of the TCO.

Return on Investment (ROI) Defined

ROI Defined: A formula to calculate the Earnings from the Investment of Capital, where the earnings are expressed as a proportion of the outlay.

Knowing the value of ROI is important when making a business investment because it clearly demonstrates the financial gains of the proposed project, compared to the relative cost.

The Return on Investment (ROI) calculation is fairly straightforward, and is defined as the ratio of the net gain from a proposed project, divided by its total costs.

In formula form, ROI is represented as:

$$ROI = \text{Cumulative net benefits} \div \text{total costs}$$

The ROI calculation uses the cumulative investment costs over the analysis period, and compares this with the total savings and other tangible benefits over the same period. The ROI value is usually expressed as a percentage, multiplying the ratio by 100%.

For example, if a project has an ROI% of 200%, the expected net benefits of the project are double those of the expected costs for implementing the project. In more basic terms, every $1 invested in the project will yield $2 in net returns.

In an analysis where the costs and benefits have been properly estimated, decision makers typically look for higher percentages for ROI as an indication of risk reduction. The higher the percentage the less risk typically, because the benefits are much higher than the costs, and the project is more tolerant if costs overrun predictions, or benefits fall short of expectations.

Benefits

Costs

ROI Calculation Example

To understand further, let us examine the cash flows from a sample project and the resultant ROI calculation:

Example Cash Flow

	Initial	Year 1	Year 2	Year 3	Cumulative Total
Total Costs	$100,000	$25,000	$25,000	$25,000	$175,000
Total Benefits		$200,000	$200,000	$200,000	$600,000
Net Benefits	$(100,000)	$175,000	$175,000	$175,000	$425,000

$$ROI (\%) = \$425,000 \div \$175,000 = 243\%$$

The ROI in this example was calculated by taking the Cumulative Net Benefits of $425,000 divided by the Cumulative Total Costs of $175,000. Hence, the net benefits are more than double the investment, yielding an ROI% of 243%. Every $1 invested will yield a $2.43 in net returns.

Limitations in Calculating ROI?

As a simple percentage calculation, ROI is easy to understand, and easy to apply to comparisons, however the ROI calculation if used as the only measure of a projects viability, has some shortcomings.

1. The ROI formula shows the net return from investment but does not indicate the time associated with achieving the returns.

2. The ROI calculation does not recognize that in some cases, the projects total cost and benefit value may be so small that the net benefits are not worth considering. As an example, the ROI% of a planned project might be a significant 500%, but the net benefits of $10,000 on a $2,000 investment are so small that the project is not worth comparing to the millions of dollars in benefit that most corporations are seeking. Conversely, for some projects the costs may be so high that even though the net benefit and ROI yield are high, the project exceeds a reasonable investment risk. For example, a project that costs $10 million and has a projected net benefit of $100M, yields an ROI% of 1000%, but the risk of applying $10 million to a single project might be too high for a cash strapped company. Thus background economic scenario of each situation must be considered.

3. The standard ROI calculation typically does not use net present value terms in its calculations. Net present value calculations use the "time value of money", which takes into account the fact that the purchasing power of a dollar received in the future is less than dollar possessed today. The ROI calculation does not take into account that many projects require up-front investments that then need to be offset by savings in outgoing years, but that these savings are not as valuable when compared to up-front costs because money in the future is worth less than today. To resolve this issue, sometimes the ROI formula includes net present value calculations for the net benefits and the costs.

The Bottom-Line

Overall, the ROI calculation provides a valuable comparison of the net benefit verses total cost, a ratio that can point towards a solution that delivers optimum financial benefits. But ROI alone is not the only indicator of whether proposed solution is a good investment. The analysis should also consider with other factors such as NPV Savings, IRR, and payback period prior to making a purchase decision.

Net Present Value (NPV) Savings Defined

NPV Definition: The sum that results when the discounted value of the expected costs of an investment are deducted from the discounted value of the expected returns.

The Net Present Value (NPV) benefit is a calculation that measures the net cash flow gains of a proposed solution in today's dollar terms, taking into account that over time money today is more valuable than money in the future.

The NPV savings calculation consists of two financial concepts:

• The "net" part of the NPV savings calculation is the difference between all costs and all benefits (savings and other gains).

• The present value portion of the NPV calculation takes into account the time value of money; so that adjusts to expenditures and returns, as they occur over time, can be evaluated equally.

When examining a proposed purchase decision, and knowing that money has a time value, future payments need to be higher than investments made today in order to be equivalent to today's dollars.

This time value accounts for the fact that:

• Money typically inflates over time, meaning that a dollar invested today will be worth less in the future because of inflation.

• A dollar invested today could earn interest over time, so the investment needs to make up for the lost opportunity. As the investment could earn interest elsewhere at the organizations weighted average the cost of capital, this is often called opportunity cost.

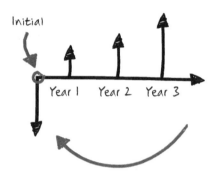
Initial
Year 1   Year 2   Year 3

NPV Defined

The NPV calculation evaluates a set of costs and benefits over time in order to account for the time value of money. The cash flows are the amounts and timings of the various investment costs and benefits, and these are brought into a common term, today's dollars, so that the net benefit can be quantified and compared if necessary to competing investment opportunities.

Using an IT project as an example, let's say that a company invests $100,000 in a new application and that the application requires $25,000 annually thereafter in maintenance and support costs. From this investment, the company expects to save $200,000 each year. An analysis of this investment over three years would yield the following negative (costs) and positive (benefit) cash flows:

Example Cash Flow

	Initial	Year 1	Year 2	Year 3	Cumulative Total
Total Costs	$100,000	$25,000	$25,000	$25,000	$175,000
Total Benefits		$200,000	$200,000	$200,000	$600,000
Net Benefits	$(100,000)	$175,000	$175,000	$175,000	$425,000

The cash flow from this investment is shown as the Net Benefit, which is the Total Benefits minus Total Costs: a cash flow of -$100,000 initially (year 0), with $175,000 in year 1, year 2 and year 3.

The NPV Savings calculation seems intimidating when expressed as a formula; however, when demonstrated in practical terms it is quite intuitive. Mathematically NPV calculation is represented by the formula:

$$NPV = I_0 + \frac{I_1}{1+r} + \frac{I_2}{(1+r)^2} + \dots + \frac{I_n}{(1+r)^n}$$

In this formula, the " I "s represent the net benefits for each year, the subscript "0" represents the initial net benefit, the subscript "1" represents the year one net benefit, and so on. The exponent in the denominator is also equal to each year of the analysis, up to n, the number of years in the analysis term. The discount rate is r and is held constant through the analysis period.

To put the calculation in practical, step-by-step terms, we will use the calculation applied against our example cash flows. The net present value calculation, using a cost of capital/discount rate of 7%, takes the initial costs and ongoing costs and benefit cash flows to create a single net cost or savings figure. For the example set of cash flows in the above table, the net benefits are as follows:

	Initial = I(0)	Year 1 = I(1)	Year 2 = I(2)	Year 3 = I(3)
Net Benefits	$(100,000)	$175,000	$175,000	$175,000

The initial expense of $100,000 is not discounted because it is already in today's dollars terms. However, Year 1 through Year 3 need to be adjusted to be brought into today's dollar terms and is calculated as follows:

NPV Year 1 = $175,000 divided by (1+ .07) = $163,551

NPV Year 2 = $175,000 divided by (1+.07) squared = $152,852

NPV Year 3 = $175,000 divided by (1+.07) cubed = $142,852

The total NPV savings is the sum of the initial expense and the three-year NPV analysis, represented as:

NPV Savings = - $100,000 + $163,551+ $152,852 + $142,852 = $ 359,255

As shown, the net benefits from later years are discounted more in today's dollar terms such that they mean less in the overall analysis. As a result, the total NPV savings is only $359,255 compared to the cumulative benefits of $425,000 when the discount rate is not considered.

The higher the discount rate is and the further into the future that a cash flow will occur, typically the lower the present value of that cash flow will be. Because the net present value calculation increases the impact of current costs and near term savings while reducing the impact of future costs or benefits, the following holds true:

• Projects with high initial costs and savings that grow slowly over time yield lower NPV savings values;

• Projects with low initial costs and greater initial savings yield higher NPV savings calculations.

The Bottom-Line

The NPV Savings is one of the most popular and accurate methods used to assess purchase decision viability. NPV uses discounted cash flow to accurately quantify the net benefits from a proposed solution.

However, the NPV calculation usually cannot be used alone to determine whether a proposed solution investment is viable. As an example, a solution may yield a substantial $100M NPV savings over a three-year period, but the required initial investment of $10M may be so risky for the company that it is not considered a prudent risk. As well, a proposed solution might have a large NPV benefit but has a long payback period and derives much of its benefits through huge gains in outgoing years.

Risk-Adjusted ROI Defined (Applying NPV to the ROI formula)

A variation on the traditional ROI formula, Risk Adjusted ROI is calculated as the ratio of the net gain from a proposed solution, divided by its total costs - represented in net present value terms to account for project risk.

This formula takes into account the time value of money and leverages NPV to generate a more accurate indicator as a result.

In a formula, this can be represented as:

$$\text{Risk Adjusted ROI} =$$

$$\text{Net Present Value of Cumulative Net Benefit} \div \text{Net Present Value of Total Costs}$$

The Risk Adjusted ROI is typically presented as a percentage which demonstrates the value of the proposed investment, and as opposed to the basic ROI formula, the benefits and costs are adjusted into net present value terms to account for lack of visibility in future cash flows.

The risk-adjusted ROI calculation is adjusted for risk by using the discount rate and net present value terms, and therefore is actually better to use than the more traditional ROI formula. However, because the basic ROI formula is easier to understand, especially for quick calculations, it is dramatically more popular, and for most proposals, good enough for the buying committee.

Payback Period Defined

Payback Period Defined: The time period from the start of the proposed purchase until the cumulative cash flow turns positive

Perhaps the easiest calculation to understand of all the financial summary metrics used in an ROI analysis is the payback period.

The payback period is defined as the time frame needed for the proposed purchase to yield a positive cumulative cash flow, which is typically specified in months. The payback period starts being measured at the beginning of a purchase decision / project and stops being measured when the cumulative benefits exceed the cumulative costs.

On a graph of cumulative benefits and costs, it is the elapsed time from project start to the point where the lines cross (see figure). This point is often referred to as the break-even point, demonstrated in this example:

Example Cash Flow

	Initial	Year 1	Year 2	Year 3	Cumulative Total
Total Costs	$100,000	$25,000	$25,000	$25,000	$175,000
Total Benefits		$200,000	$200,000	$200,000	$600,000
Net Benefits	$(100,000)	$175,000	$175,000	$175,000	$425,000

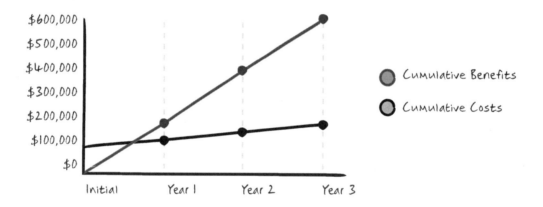

The Bottom-Line

Payback period is important because it measures how long it takes for an investment to begin generating a positive cash flow. A longer payback period generates risk, especially if the project time line is delayed or benefits occur later than expected. A shorter payback period does not guarantee substantial returns for the investment; instead, it assures that there will be positive returns and that the benefits will occur early in the cycle and quickly offset the initial investment costs.

As with other financial summary metrics, payback period has its issues if used alone, such as failing to communicate the value of returns, only the time to returns. But as a measure of risk and speed to reward, it serves as one of the best early indicators as to the speed of potential rewards a project can deliver.

In today's frugal environment, payback measurement on projects is a requirement, and fast payback mandatory - typically dictated as 12 months or less from the proposed solution's deployment.

Comparing and Selecting Solutions Using TCO Analysis

"TCO is defined as the total cost of procuring, using, managing and disposing of an asset over its useful life." – Bill Kirwin, the Father of TCO, Gartner

Total Cost of Ownership (TCO) refers to a useful accounting system to tally all of the costs associated with a given asset over its entire useful life. Costs are tallied for planning, acquisition, setup & installation, manage & support, evolution and retirement.

For buyers, TCO helps to make better decisions going beyond the original purchase costs, to include total lifecycle costs such as service contracts, management and support, power and cooling, facilities space costs, evolution, and retirement costs.

For sellers, TCO provides an account of all costs for various solutions and options, helping vendors compare and contrast their proposed solutions with others / competitors, proving which solutions are not only less expensive up-front, but less expensive in total cost over time.

TCO was born in the late 1980s by Bill Kirwin of Gartner, used to initially compare the costs of mainframe / minicomputers with PCs and networks. In these studies of early IT investments, the purchase price of the hardware and software was found to be only 15% of the total cost of owning the asset. Management, direct support and hidden user support accounted for 85% of the total cost over the useful life of the asset. At the time, a PC that cost $2,000 to $3,000 might actually cost the organization over $8,000 per year or more to keep in service.

TCO is most useful when comparing different solution options, to determine which provides the lowest total cost of ownership.

To do this, TCO first creates/uses an accounting system to tally all costs for the solutions being compared, when done correctly assuring that no costs are overlooked. The accounting system is called the "Chart of Accounts".

Typical TCO Chart of Accounts

Direct Costs (budgeted)

Hardware and Software	$1,903
Management	#1,345
Support	$1,094
Development	$345
Communications	$610
Total Direct Costs	$5,305

Indirect Costs (unbudgeted)

End User Operations	$3,357
Downtime	$830
Total Indirect Costs	$4,187

Annual TCO per User: $9,493

Total Costs over 3 Years

Direct Costs (budgeted)	Desktop PCs	Virtual Desktops
Hardware and Software	$740	$790
Management	$1,259	$790
Support	$1,434	$440
Networking	$75	$335
Total Direct Costs	$3,508	$2355

Indirect Costs (unbudgeted)		
Self / Peer Support	$980	$150
Downtime	$440	$150
Total Indirect Costs	$1,420	$150

Annual TCO per User:	$4,928	$2,655

Second, for all the solutions being compared, the costs are tallied for each cost category. Placing these costs in the chart of accounts and comparing them head to head illustrates where some solutions are more expensive than others. Totaling the costs for each solution and comparing the totals indicates the lowest total cost solution.

When comparing solutions, TCO only shows a portion of the decision-making criteria. TCO is focused on costs, but places little on comparing the different business value of the asset. For example, to lower the TCO of productivity tools for users, desktop computers could be replaced with pen and pad, which has a TCO of $1.50, compared to an estimated $3,000 per year for the typical Microsoft Windows computer system.

As Lenny Liebmann of ComputerWorld indicates, "Lower TCO doesn't mean higher ROI: This is a classic error. The assumption is that if you whittle down the cost of a resource, it will provide a higher return on investment. Not! If I buy a cheap used car and lose my job because I can't get to work reliably, did I really save money? Sure, IT must control costs, but not through some arbitrary goal that isn't linked to real business drivers."

Rightly so, by focusing on costs alone, the dramatic benefit differences of and between proposed solutions could be overlooked. It is therefore important to compare not just the TCO of different solutions, but the ROI differences as well (where ROI takes into account total cost of ownership versus benefits for each proposed solution).

Cap-Ex vs. Op Ex

When a prospect considers investing in your solution, it is likely they will give consideration not just to the costs and benefits, but the different accounting classifications of the cost / benefits as well, particularly the unique treatment between capital expenditures (Cap-Ex) and operating expenses (Op-Ex).

A **capital expenditure** is an investment to acquire or improve an asset, usually a physical piece of equipment. Much of the cost for the asset will then be charged to depreciation **expense** over the useful life of the asset.

For example, you are selling a new medical imaging system to a hospital. The hospital plans to purchase the asset, and it will be recorded as a capital expenditure. The hospital will have a cash outlay initially to purchase the equipment. Because the asset will be depreciated, a tax benefit is also generated each year.

An **operating expense** is an ongoing business cost for running a product, business, or system.

For example, you are proposing a Cloud computing solution. The monthly fee for the service is an operating expense, and doesn't require the business group to invest in on-premise compute infrastructure and software. The investment is a simple monthly fee charged to the business, and often classified as an operating expense.

For many organizations considering different proposals, it is harder to get capital expenditures approved. The capital expenditure affects the company's balance sheet, adding an asset to the books. On the other hand, most business units have much discretion over their operating expenses, making it easier to consider and approve such investments.

When it comes to benefits, the opposite is true. Retiring a capital asset that has not been fully depreciated has a write-down cost of the remaining depreciation that will reduce the proposed benefit (which is usually a reduction in the operating expenses related to the asset). If your solution delivers Op-ex benefits, these don't have depreciation impacts, and provide a direct contribution to the bottom-line.

Classification of different costs / benefits between Cap-Ex and Op-Ex is not always straight-forward. There are complex rules regarding leases and software that often make what appears to be clear, less so regarding accounting classification.

If a proposed solution is a significant capital expenditure, such as comparing lease vs. buy, or displacing a large legacy asset, you likely need to factor Cap-Ex and Op-Ex accounting into your financial justification. If this is not the case, we suggest avoiding the accounting / tax complexity – focusing on simple justification to support your value story (versus getting into deep accounting discussions and analysis).

THREE VALUE CONVERSATIONS

Your value conversation will evolve — depending on where your buyer is in their decision-making process. Here are examples of what three value conversations would look like in the real world:

Quantify the Pain for Early-Stage Prospects (Why Change?)

Do you know exactly how much your downtime is costing you? Research indicates that:

• The majority of Fortune 500 companies (59%) experiences an average of 1.6 hours of downtime each week (D&B)

• Each hour of downtime costs an average of $181,000 in recovery costs, lost productivity and impacted business revenue (Aberdeen)

Based on the issues you've uncovered, you have at least one downtime event each month with about an hour to recover from each issue. Each downtime hour costs you $1M, which makes your downtime costs much higher than the national average.

With 12 hours of downtime each year, these issues cost you an estimated $12 million in recovery labor, lost user productivity and partner/customer business impacts annually.

With such a large cost, improving availability should be a big priority. Do you agree?

Justify the Gain for Middle-Stage Prospects (Why Now?)

With our solution, you can improve your availability. Case studies of companies similar to yours, confirmed by IDC research, reveal that you can reduce your downtime by 50%.

Applying this to your organization means reducing your downtime to less than six hours a year and saving $6M.

Prove You're Not the Same for Late-Stage Prospects (Why You?)

Our solution delivers this business value with superior results and at a much lower TCO than other options.

IDC reports that because we are software as a service, you can save $500,000 a year in licensing, infrastructure, management and support costs compared to the competitive on-premise solutions.

Our unique features of X, Y and Z also help us deliver superior availability results without incremental costs.

Pathos: Stimulate Emotions

Pathos aligns with the Reptilian Brain. This is the most ancient part of the brain, thought to have evolved over 400 million years ago.

The Reptilian Brain is responsible for survival – subconsciously processing our environment and reacting to keep us alive. Think of how territorial reptiles are and how quickly they react to danger. **It's about fight or flight.**

To get buyers to pay attention, you must move beyond logic and stimulate the Reptilian Brain. Since the Reptilian Brain is all about survival, its hyper-responsive to visuals.

Visuals can make buyers take notice and your sales conversations memorable. Research from Rain has shown that people only remember about 10% of what you say after 48 hours. However, **when you attach a simple visual to your message, people will remember 65% of what you say.**

This is because the brain needs to interpret words but it immediately connects with imagery.

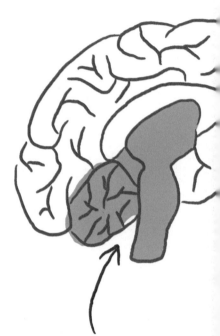

Basal ganglia / Reptilian brain

How Visuals Make Stories Memorable

Visuals hold the key to effective value communications.

Research shows that visuals can stimulate attention, decrease learning time, improve comprehension, enhance retrieval and increase retention. When you combine great visuals with a great story, you'll see dramatic results.

Why are visuals so important?

Most of our brain is dedicated to vision. According to William G. Allyn, Professor of Medical Optics at the University of Rochester, "More than 50 percent of the cortex, the surface of the brain, is devoted to processing visual information." This is compared with an estimated eight percent for touch and just three percent for hearing.

By attaching a visual, people will remember seven times more from your conversation.

If you try to communicate value using just verbal communications, your words will not have a lasting impact.

According to Psychology Today, "a study asked students to remember many groups of three words each, such as dog, bike and street. Students who tried to remember the words by repeating them over and over again did poorly on recall."

Visuals can also make your written communications more effective. According to the Psychology Today study, "Words are abstract and rather difficult for the brain to retain, whereas visuals are concrete and, as such, more easily remembered."

When you add visuals to your spoken or written words, you can dramatically increase your audience's recall. A study from California State University has shown that people remember 10% of spoken communications and 20% of visual communications. But when you combine oral and visual communications, your audience will remember more than 80% of what you say.

Researchers at the Wharton School of Business compared visual presentations with purely verbal presentations. Sixty-seven percent of the study's participants felt that the presenters who used visuals were more persuasive.

Why are visuals and oral communications so effective when they are combined? Research indicates that there are two (or more) distinct cognitive systems for processing verbal versus visual information. When the brain processes these together, people can store information in two forms. This is called dual-coding, involving both verbal and visual memory. Research has found that recall, retention and understanding all improve when graphics and words are processed together.

Are all visual communications created equal? Research suggests that visuals are more effective when they allow readers to "interpret and integrate information with minimum cognitive processing". Think about cave drawings or illustrations from children's books – they are simple line drawings with clear colors.

ORAL AND VISUAL INFORMATION: PERCENTAGE RETAINED

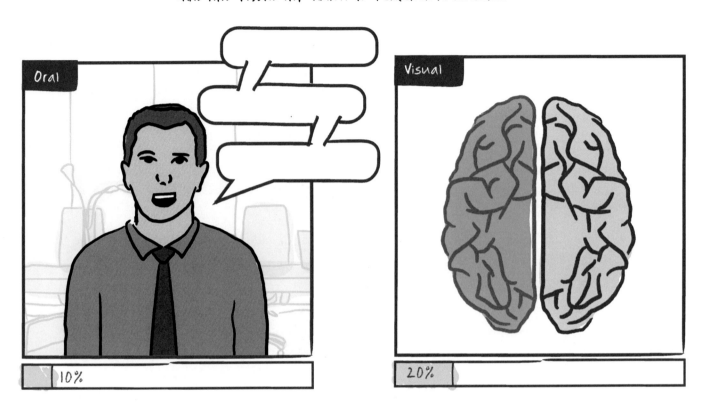

Contrast

So, what types of visuals are the most effective?

Our Reptilian Brain requires contrast for cognition.

Picture this ...

You have a large pot of boiling water on the stove. You take a big, green frog and throw it in the boiling water. The frog's survival instinct kicks in, and it jumps out of the pot.

Now imagine that you fill the pot with tap water at room temperature. You put the frog in the pot and slowly increase the temperature. The frog doesn't realize that it's in any danger and soon you have frog soup.

So, without contrast, you won't stimulate the reptilian brain or get a response. With contrast, you'll get an immediate response.

The best way to communicate contrast is to show "a day in the life" of one of your customers, documenting their work environment and the challenges they face each day. Use simple and visual examples to paint a picture. Show the challenges, risks and costs your customer faced before they started using your solution. Then, highlight how much better things are with your solution.

How to use "Before-and-after" Stories to Show Value

Contrast is used to highlight what the buyer's life is like under the current situation (before) compared to how it will be improved after purchasing your solution (after).

This technique is frequently used in consumer advertising – just think of all the weight loss ads with before-and-after stories. One reason why these ads work is because they have compelling visuals.

An effective way to show a before and after is to make your customer the hero in your story. Show how not only their business – but their life – was improved by using your solution.

Here's an example from Splunk:

a. Before: Support calls went through a very complex process. They would come into the service desk and the engineering scrum. Then, Splunk would try to determine an issue's root cause amongst a scrum of engineers and islands of management – along with support logs from applications, servers, virtualization and more.

b. After: In contrast, a support call comes to the support desk. A support person immediately searches a centralized big data repository that's consolidated from all of Splunk's applications, devices and systems.

Using before-and-after stories lets prospects:

• Clearly visualize how their current situation (before) is full of complexity, issues, costs and risks.

• Learn how much better the after can be, and how much simpler their life will become.

• See the differences between the before and after, which will motivate them to move away from the status quo and choose your solution.

When you develop visuals to show contrast, look for the following:

• Be sure the "before" aligns with the key challenges your buyer has and demonstrates the costs and risks in sticking with business as usual.

• Make the "after" clear and concise, as the buyer may latch on to the un-certainty in the before visualization and stick with the status quo.

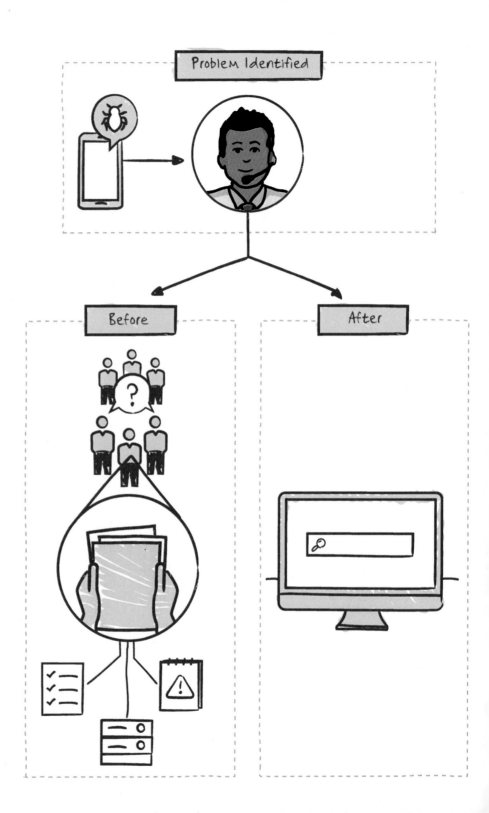

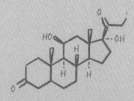

Cortisol, which signals and maintains engagement and focus, helping the audience pay attention

Oxytocin, which deepens the level of engagement and creates a feeling of empathy

Storytelling

In addition to visuals and contrast, you should also add storytelling to your mix. Storytelling goes back to our primitive roots and appeals to the Reptilian Brain. Cave drawings, Oscar-winning movies and classic novels all have told stories that stood the test of time.

The first key to a successful story is making your buyer the hero. Many companies only talk about how great their products and services are. They position their sales team as heroes. However, if you want your story to resonate with buyers, you must take the focus off your company and put it on your customers.

The second key to a successful story is knowing where to include the juiciest parts. The Reptilian Brain is most likely to recall what happens at the beginning and end of story, so this is where you should include your most important information.

The Storytelling Arc

"Storytelling" is big in B2B marketing and sales. It leads buyers down a path and helps them realize that they need your solution.

In this age of Frugalnomics, your ability to communicate your value is more important than ever. This means that the quality of your stories can make or break or your sales.

If you tell your value story the wrong way, you'll bore prospects, and they won't respond to your messages. However, a well-crafted value story can have a powerful effect on prospects and literally ignite their buying decisions.

What does this mean for your B2B marketing and sales strategies?

In a world of shorter attention spans and increased skepticism, you need to create memorable value stories. Creating an epic value story doesn't mean spending millions on a splashy ad campaign. It means explaining your value in a way that resonates with your buyers on a business, personal and emotional level. Your value story should excite buyers' senses as they see that you understand their challenges and can solve their business issues.

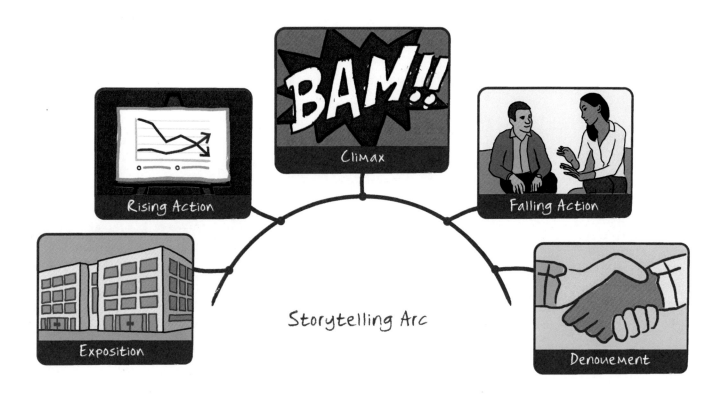

Storytelling Arc

According to neuroscience research, an effective story must unfold in a specific manner. It should contain a "dramatic arc" that includes the following key elements:

• Exposition   • Rising action   • Climax   • Falling action   • Denouement

The **Exposition** sets the story's stage and provides important background information. In your value story, this means outlining the **business challenges** your buyer faces on a daily basis. You can do this with "a day in the life" stories.

The **Rising Action** of a story builds suspense and captures the reader's interest. This is where you detail the perils of the status quo and the "**cost of doing nothing**". Show the detrimental effects of not taking action.

The storytelling arc is also referred to as Freytag's Pyramid, after 19th century playwright Gustav Freytag. While not an entirely new idea at the time, Freytag cemented the concepts of a five-act play in his book, Die Technik des Dramas.

The benefits of this five-part structure reach far beyond the stage. Authors, film makers, and artists continue to use this format to deliver powerful stories.

In the **Climax** of a story we experience the turning point and see a glimmer of hope for the future. To make your value story impactful, discuss what's possible – the '**what if**' – and paint a picture of the solution that will change your prospect's fortunes for the better.

The **Falling Action** of a story contains any unresolved tensions that need closure. It contains a great deal of suspense, as the conclusion is still in doubt. In a successful value story, your prospect's business challenges begin to ease as you discuss how the solution will save the day. However, you must also indicate risks if they take the wrong path. This is where you outline how the solution can overcome the issues, and the **benefits** of your specific solution.

The **Denouement** is the powerful ending of the story where characters resolve their issues. In an effective business story, this is where you drive it home and deliver relevant **proof points** that remove the risk. You can prove your value with case studies and testimonials.

How well are you telling your value story?

Is it crafted and delivered in a way that stimulates your buyer's brain? Does it follow the storytelling arc for the best effect? When you follow the storytelling arc and tell memorable stories, you can cause chemical changes in your prospects' brains and ignite their internal "buy buttons".

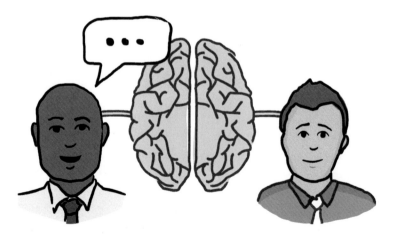

MRI studies indicate that the brain patterns of a storyteller dramatically influence the brain patterns of the listener, actually shaping the brain waves to match their own! (New Scientist)

COMMUNICATING VALUE WITH SUCCESS STORIES

To be effective, a success story needs to:

Match the prospect's
business, role and challenges.

Show how the solution helped drive
tangible business improvements and
personal achievements.

Include third-party
validation.

Client Success Story: Jowat

Project launched in 3 weeks and under budget, Reports are
180x faster

" With SAP CO-PA Accelerator powered by
SAP HANA and SAP SAP® Consulting
organization BusinessObjects Explorer,
report generation is dramatically faster and
we can standardize reporting down to the
departmental level. "

Christine Künne, CIO, Jowat AG

Benefits

Launch of SAP CO-PA Accelerator in 3 weeks and under budget

180x faster report generation from 30 – 40 minutes to 10 seconds

Improved productivity and data accuracy

Here is a good success story example and
what makes it effective:

1. It contains simple visuals.

2. The photo of the customer helps the reader connect
with the story.

3. A quote explains the benefits in the customer's own
words.

4. The tangible, quantifiable benefits clearly show the
positive outcomes.

This story would likely appeal to prospects who face time-to-market and productivity challenges. Since the
customer in this example is a CIO, other technology leaders might find the story relevant. The story may also
appeal to European prospects, since the featured customer is German.

Ethos: Appeal to Credibility

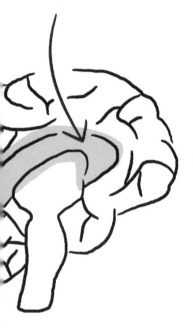

Limbic brain /
Middle brain

Ethos is related to the Middle Brain, or limbic brain. It's associated with social interactions, nurturing behaviors and mutual reciprocity.

The limbic brain is also connected to the digestive system and is responsible for the **gut feelings** we get when making decisions. Some believe the Middle Brain is the boss who has the final say in whether a prospect will say "yes" or "no" to your proposal.

To win business, you must appeal to the Middle Brain. It's not enough to capture buyers' attention and convince them that your solution is the logical choice. You must also prove that you're credible, so their gut feeling tells them to say, "yes".

See Themselves in the Outcome

Buyers can smell BS a mile away and won't always believe your claims. To close deals, you must convince buyers that your solution will deliver its promised value.

Success stories back up your claims. These stories can be in the form of case studies, video testimonials or product reviews. A compelling success story will draw your prospect in, so they visualize themselves achieving the same results as your featured customer: case studies / success stories aligned to customers just like them. The closer you can come to the prospect's industry, location, size, role, and even gender and age, the better.

Provide proof points with evidence that your benefits are tangible and achievable.

Concrete Value

Today's prospects are risk adverse and frugal, so it's important to document any benefits you can help them achieve. This includes showing prospects the costs of doing nothing, as well as any savings you can help them achieve. Your case studies should mention tangible benefits such as KPI's, top line and bottom line improvements. Don't be abstract, as this will make it difficult to appeal to the limbic brain.

Also show prospects the professional and personal successes that their peers have achieved. This helps them visualize themselves as successful. Create case studies that align with their industry, location, company size and role. The more you can diversify your case studies, the more prospects will see themselves as your happy customer.

Third Party Validation

Only 13% of buyers view vendor-created content as credible. To boost your credibility, you need validation from third parties. Provide buyers with content that your customers and fans are creating – such as reviews, insights and success stories.

Taking these steps will help you give prospects that "warm and fuzzy feeling" that they are making the right decision by partnering with you.

Only 13% of buyers view vendor-created content as credible. To boost your credibility, you need validation from third parties.

It's All Greek to Me

"There's two kinds of people: Greeks and everybody else who wish they were Greeks" (Gus Portokalos from My Big Fat Greek Wedding) .

To ignite buying decisions, you need to be Greek ... or at least think like one! For the best sales and marketing results, take a cue from Aristotle and modern neuroscience. Ensure that your messaging addresses:

1. Logos and the New Brain

2. Pathos and the Reptilian Brain

3. Ethos and the Middle Brain.

If you leave one of these three out, you won't get the best results.

PONOS AND CHRONOS — MORE ANCIENT KEYS TO MODERN SALES SUCCESS?

At a recent sales training, I had the pleasure of having Demetrios Miras in the class. Being of Greek heritage, Demetrios approached me after the session to tell me how much he liked the discussions about Aristotle, and how proud he was about how much the ancient Greeks could teach us about modern selling.

Indeed, 2,600 years ago Aristotle taught us three important ways to "win friends and influence people," and amazingly, these three ancient "selling" techniques align perfectly with the three "buy buttons" of the brain, as revealed by modern neuroscience:

1. Logos (Logic) and the New brain (Neocortex) — use of reasoning to convince your buyer and the conscious portion of their decision-making, that the purchase is rational. Financial justification is vital to win over your buyer, proving that the "cost of do nothing" is untenable and the return on investment (ROI) is substantial and quick.

2. Pathos (Emotion) and the Reptilian Brain (Cerebellum) — use of simple visuals, contrast and storytelling to gain the buyer's emotional connection to your conversations and proposals, making you more memorable, gaining empathy and sparking action.

3. Ethos (Trust) and the Middle Brain — use of success stories, references, 3rd party validation to provide a positive "gut feel", gaining credibility and impressing on the buyer that you are someone worth listening to, and are trustworthy to buy from.

Demtrious pointed out that Aristotle had even more wisdom to impart, with two more important "purchase motivators" that sales reps could further leverage in their conversations and proposals:

Ponos (Pain) — In this "do more with less" economy, your prospects are under extreme budget and resource pressure, and are often struggling to just "keep the lights on" versus considering new innovative projects. Often your prospects aren't fully aware of the issues you are trying to help them address. As a result, a good amount of your conversations and proposal content needs to focus, not on your solution and its benefits, but educating and proving that the status quo pain / need has to be addressed. Success means assuring you are aligned with known issues and helping to make these a priority, while helping to uncover issues that could be costly if not addressed. The key: helping the buyer answer the question "Why Change?" by illuminating the "Pain."

Chronos (Time Period) — it is important to not only convince a buyer that they should change from the status quo (Why Change?), and that you are worth buying from (Why You?), but to convince them that waiting is not an option (Why Now?). Making the buyer conscious of Chronos, that time is money, is imperative to winning and accelerating the purchase decision. Your prospects don't have unlimited budget and resources, and your proposal is not the only one they are considering. You have to convince the prospect that your proposed project is a priority above all others, and that every day / week / month of delay has a tangible cost.

In the movie My Big Fat Greek Wedding, the bride's Dad, Gus Portokalos would always say that "the Greeks invented everything", and as I learn more about Aristotle and what he can teach us about modern selling (let alone Plato), Gus may have been right, and certainly Demetrios Miras has much to be proud of with his heritage.

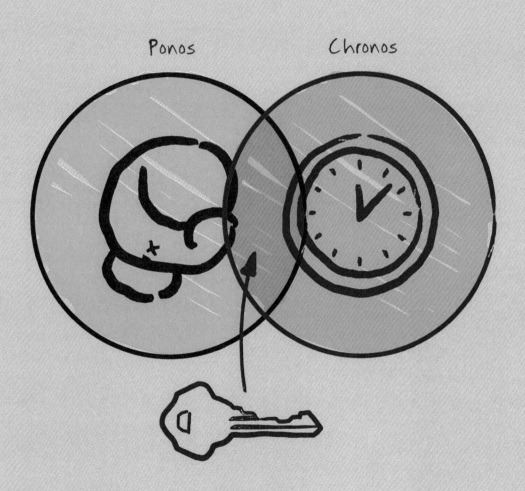

The CLOSE Conversation Guide: Bringing It All Together in a Value Story

The CLOSE Conversation Guide is a framework to help you formulate your value proposition so you can effectively articulate it. The guide incorporates each of Aristotle's persuasions and buying brains. It also includes the five key elements you should articulate – in order – for proven best effect. These five elements are **Challenge, Loss, Opportunity, Solution and Evidence (CLOSE).**

Let's look at each of these elements and how they can help you develop and communicate your unique value story:

Challenge	Loss
What Challenge Can You Help Prospects Tackle?	**What are the challenges currently costing?**
Help uncover challenges that your prospects may not realize they have. You can also help prospects understand the implications of known challenges that may not yet be a priority.	Quantify the specific "cost of doing nothing" for the prospect. What is maintaining the status quo costing the organization?
Illustrate the seriousness of the challenge with compelling commercial insights as to how prevalent the issue is, along with what it costs an average company to ignore the issue.	Tally the current "do nothing" costs as: • Unnecessary expenses • Lost productivity / inefficient or error-prone processes • Potential risks and risk-related losses • Lost revenue and growth opportunities
Communicate ways that the challenge typically manifests itself (use examples from your other customers). This paints a picture of a day in the life when you maintain the status quo.	Quantify the specific "cost of doing nothing" for the prospect. What is maintaining the status quo costing the organization?

Opportunity	Solution	Evidence

What is the value of addressing the challenge?

What solution can deliver these business benefits?

How can I be assured that the proposed solution can deliver?

Communicate the potential business benefits of solving the issue outlined in the challenge.

Document specific solutions that can address the particular prospect challenges and deliver the proposed business benefits.

Validate how similar customers have successfully used the proposed solutions. Discuss the tangible business and personal value they achieved.

Tally the impact to specific business metrics or value drivers.

Communicate the differentiating features of the solution. These should impact the value drivers and result in significant business benefits – proving how the value is uniquely delivered.

Quantify specific customer benefits, tallying KPI impacts, financial business benefits and ROI.

Quantify the following business results using the Value Map™:

- Cost savings and avoidance

- Improved productivity and business processes

- Reduced risks

- Improved revenue growth

Filter the evidence by industry, size and role to better resonate with prospects. This shows prospects that they can reap similar business and personal rewards.

Using the CLOSE Conversation Guide helps prospects see you as a trusted advisor – not a pushy vendor. This will improve your sales results so you can close more deals and drive revenue.

You can use the CLOSE Conversation Guide to improve all your customer conversations, applying the methodology to develop:

• Provocative prospecting emails (use one line in the email to cover each element in CLOSE)

• More impactful and personalized white papers and infographics (using the elements of CLOSE to drive the content)

• High impact in-person or online meetings (evolving from one-size-fits-all PowerPoint pitches to communicating the best value story for each prospect)

The beauty of CLOSE is that it ties together all the elements we just discussed (e.g. Ethos, Pathos and Logos / New, Reptilian and Middle Brains). CLOSE also:

• Puts the buyer first. It focuses on the buyer's challenges – not your solution. CLOSE also helps you quantify the cost of "do nothing" and value of change.

• Uses visuals and "before and after" stories to engage buyers.

• Follows the storytellers arc, placing the most important elements at the beginning and end of the story.

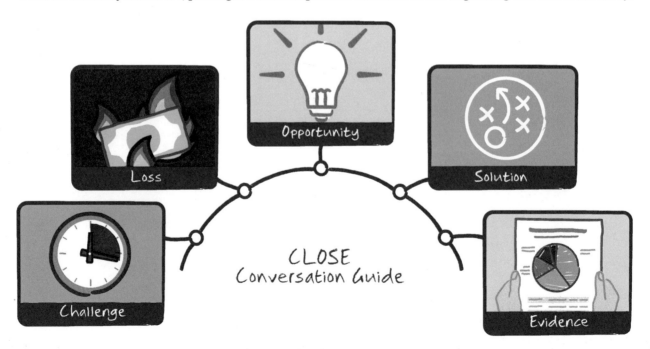

SURVIVAL TIPS

1

Be sure all conversations and communications use Aristotle's art of persuasion and address each of the brain's "buying buttons".

2

Convince the New Brain with logic. State the prospect's business benefits according to the Value Map™. Align your conversations with the buyer's roles, challenges and stage in the sales cycle.

3

Stimulate the Reptilian Brain with emotions. Use visuals, contrast and storytelling

4

Comfort the Middle Brain with credibility. Help buyers "see themselves in the results." Make your value concrete and personal. Ensure that a third party certifies your results.

5

Organize the conversation according to the CLOSE messaging methodology (Challenge, Loss, Opportunity, Solution and Evidence)

ΑΡΙΣΤΟΤΕΛΗΣ

ADP Launches Value Campaign To Boost Pipelines by $1 Million in Just Three Months

"Value selling has changed the way that we sell. We now have tools that make our sales reps more consultative, so they can provide clients with greater value."

Patrick Flanigan
VP, Sales Enablement, ADP

The Challenge: Help Customers See ADP As More Than Just a Payroll Company

Many people think that ADP just does payroll.

However, ADP offers a wealth of human capital management (HCM) services to help clients build a better workforce. These services include human resources, talent management, benefits administration and more.

"We're trying to shift our branding to help clients see us as an integrated HCM provider," said Patrick Flanigan, vice president, sales lead generation. "We offer these services to employers of all sizes – from small businesses to enterprises."

For the past few years, ADP's sales team has been quantifying the value of a full suite of services. They performed TCO comparisons on a complete solution versus point solutions. To do this, ADP had separate spreadsheets that crunched the numbers but weren't easy to use.

It was difficult for sales to formalize the process across multiple spreadsheets, improve adoption and get reps clear on ADP's messaging.

"Our sales team needed a central tool that would help them explain ADP's value in a consistent way - regardless of which line of business they are speaking with," said Flanigan .

In addition, many of ADP's prospects wanted to explore solutions on their own before engaging with a sales rep. ADP didn't have a way to enable prospects to research the value of these services on their own.

The Losses: Approximately 60% of ADP's Deals Were Stalling

The lack of consistent value communication and quantification made it difficult for ADP to close deals.

Approximately 60% of ADP's opportunities stalled. Marketing found it difficult to advance opportunities and sales reps had trouble getting second meetings.

This was particularly an issue with mid-market and enterprise sales, when ADP was in a competitive environment and faced a complex buying process with more decision makers and steps.

The Opportunity: Provide Clients with Valuable HCM Insights to Drive Opportunities and Sales

To drive sales, ADP needed the right materials to guide clients through the decision-making process – whether they were researching ADP's HCM solutions online or meeting face to face with a sales rep.

ADP saw an opportunity to create a value-based tool that would allow prospects to assess and benchmark their current HCM practices, gaining insights into their priority issues. Prospects could use the marketing tool "self-service" from ADP's website. This would help position ADP as a thought leader in HCM and motivate clients to prioritize the challenges that ADP could best solve – moving them from "do nothing" to "yes."

"We saw that if we could give clients a personalized snapshot of their business, we had more valuable conversations," said Flanigan. "However, ADP didn't have a way to make this easy for clients. We also lacked the right data points and didn't know how to best articulate the message."

The Solution: The HCM Challenge

ADP conducted an extensive search for vendors who could assist with its value messaging and the development of a diagnostic assessment / financial justification tool.

"We chose a vendor who was uniquely positioned to help us show value in a complicated B2B situation," said Flanigan. "They combined the messaging with the tools to provide a complete value-based selling approach."

Approximately 60% of ADP's opportunities stalled. Marketing found it difficult to advance opportunities and sales reps had trouble getting second meetings.

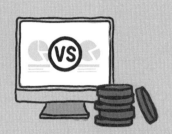

Within the first three months, the HCM Challenge tool generated over $1 million in new sales opportunities and $250,000 in wins.

The HCM Challenge tool and campaign were born from these efforts. The challenge was designed to engage prospects online and also had a follow-up program from sales reps.

The demand generation and lead nurturing campaign consisted of an interactive white paper that helped prospects achieve a basic understanding of their unique HCM challenges and quantified the benefits they could gain from ADP's services. Prospects were then prompted - either on their own or in partnership with a sales rep - to run a diagnostic assessment. This tool measured and scored their current HCM capability, identified issues, provided intelligent recommendations and gave them financial justification. All of this information was delivered in a personalized report.

"One of our ongoing challenges was combining the right content and data into a story that sales reps could walk buyers through," said Flanigan. "The HCM Challenge not only told our story but also gave prospects a completely personalized experience."

Flanigan also recommended using technology that integrates with your existing systems to make your move to value-led selling more seamless. The HCM Challenge interfaced with Eloqua, so ADP could share new leads in real time, answer discovery questions and view the personalized reports. This integration helped to automate ADP's lead capturing and nurturing. Sales reps could also use the customer intelligence and reports for more poignant follow-up.

The Evidence: ADP Boosts Pipeline by $1 Million and Gets $250,000 in Wins Within the First Three Months

Soon after launch, the HCM Challenge provided ADP with a quick payback and significant ROI. In the first three months, the tool generated over $1 million in new sales opportunities and $250,000 in wins.

The HCM Challenge continues to bring prospects into ADP's funnel and helps nurture those opportunities throughout the buyers' journey.

ADP has found that leads coming through the HCM Challenge tool are of higher value than other leads and more likely to close deals. The HCM Challenge produces more than 150 analyses each month and has at least a $1.5 million impact on ADP's annual revenue. It remains one of the top ADP sales and marketing campaigns of all times.

The new diagnostic approach has also helped ADP decrease its stalled deals from 60% to around 30%.

This is because prospects have the diagnostics to know which issues they should address, why the issue should be a priority and the business value ADP can deliver. Sales reps also have more consultative insights to engage prospects and motivate them to advance through the purchase process.

"Value selling has changed the way that we sell," said Flanigan. "We now have tools that make our sales reps more consultative, so they can provide clients with greater value."

Besides helping ADP achieve its sales and revenue goals, the HCM Challenge tool won a prestigious Killer Content award from Demand-Gen Report at their Content2Conversion conference. This has helped Flanigan's group achieve one of its personal goals – being publicly recognized for its innovation and achievements.

Results of the Solution

- Boosts pipeline by $1 million and gets $250,000 in wins within the first three months

- Produces more than 150 new analyses for prospects each month

- Helped ADP decrease its stalled deals from 60% to around 30%.

VALUE MESSAGING

VALUE MARKETING

VALUE SELLING

VALUE TRAINING & COACHING

VALUE MANAGEMENT OFFICE

Move From Product Pitching to Value

In today's competitive B2B market, it's difficult to distinguish yourself on the basis of your company, product, service or price. The vendors who excel are those who sell and market better than the rest, as well as deliver a better customer experience.

However, most B2B sellers are missing the mark by pitching their products versus marketing and selling their value. They're not meeting the minimum expectations of today's prospects, much less delivering a superior experience.

Delivering a better experience begins and ends with the customer conversation – the precious time sales reps spend with prospects or early in the buyer's journey when your marketing content is doing the speaking for you. The key question to ask is, "Is my content marketing and are my sales reps effectively articulating and delivering value in each conversation?"

Jim Ninivaggi — Service Director, Sales Enablement Strategies, SiriusDecisions

Research indicates that customer experience is vital for differentiation and getting the buyer to advance to "Yes". **It's crucial to close the Value Gap, and more effectively communicate and quantify your value.**

In other words, it's time to change the marketing and sales conversation.

This means evolving your content marketing and empowering your sales reps to clearly articulate your value and provide a superior customer experience. To succeed at this, you must put all five of the following elements in place:

1. Value messaging to help define your unique value. This also provides the framework for articulating and quantifying your value in your content marketing, sales rep conversations and proposals.

2. Value marketing to evolve from traditional white papers and product-focused marketing content to value-centric, personalized messaging that makes your content stand out from the crowd. This also makes your marketing more relevant, memorable and effective.

3. Value selling tools to provide reps with guidance on the right value messaging and quantification. These interactive presentation tools will help sales reps elevate the customer experience.

4. Value training and coaching to give sales reps the skills and confidence they need to use your value messaging and tools. This will help them have more effective conversations with customers.

5. A value management office to tie the program together within your company and provide reps with coaching and support to ensure their success.

Read on to discover how to bring these elements into your sales and marketing conversations, so you can move from pitching products to providing value.

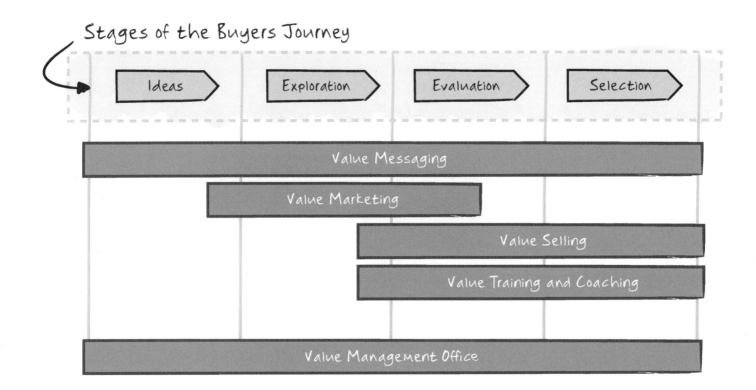

Stages of the Buyers Journey

| Ideas | Exploration | Evaluation | Selection |

Value Messaging

Value Marketing

Value Selling

Value Training and Coaching

Value Management Office

Value Messaging

Value Matrix: The Framework For Articulating Your Unique Value

The Value Matrix uses the wisdom of Aristotle's art of persuasion – along with the CLOSE conversation methodology – to create a framework of the value messaging, insights and quantification to use in different marketing and selling scenarios.

The Value Matrix helps you craft and deliver the right value storytelling, insights and quantification. For example:

• Marketing uses the Value Matrix to fuel value-focused and more effective content marketing.

• Sales uses it to guide more provocative, value-focused conversations.

Your messaging must be challenge-centric, not product-centric. It should start with your buyer's specific objectives, what they want their business to accomplish and their challenges around achieving those objectives. To determine the top business objectives, use the Value Map categories of lowering costs, improving productivity, increasing process efficiencies, mitigating business risks and driving revenue growth. You should address at least one major challenge, although your prospects will likely have several key challenges that are preventing them from achieving each objective.

Value is in the eye of the beholder, and each buyer has a unique "point of value".

It's critical to guide sales reps so they can understand the buyer's challenge and communicate your value. Give reps the right discovery questions to ask. Also provide them with content that helps them discuss the buyer's challenges and the value of overcoming these challenges.

To fuel the conversation, provide reps with unique "soundbites" and dialogue for each challenge. For example: Do you have any research around each challenge? What is the cost of doing nothing? How can I benefit from implementing the proposed solution? What is the value? Do you have evidence of business value from customers who are just like me?

Your messaging must be challenge-centric, not product-centric. It should start with specific buyer challenges around high costs, lost productivity, process inefficiencies, business risks and revenue growth constraints. From there, you can talk about potential solutions and benefits.

Jim Ninivaggi
Service Director, Sales Enablement Strategies,
SiriusDecisions

The horizontal axis of the Value Matrix includes business objectives, challenges and the relevant roles for each challenge. The vertical axis of the Value Matrix includes the CLOSE messaging for each challenge (i.e. challenge, loss, opportunity, solution and evidence).

The value messaging should follow the CLOSE messaging methodology for structuring the conversation. It should address the challenge first and move through all the CLOSE storytelling elements. For each challenge you can help the buyer address, you should provide the following value messaging:

- **Challenge.** Ask, "Did you know?" and mention recent industry research and insights.

- **Loss.** What does their situation look like now? What is doing nothing costing them?

- **Opportunity.** Show the "what if." Paint a picture of how the prospect's business and personal life will improve after they implement the proposed solution.

- **Solution.** Discuss how you can help. How will your solution help them achieve their vision? What can they save when they use your solution? Quantify the business value.

- **Evidence.** Show how you have helped similar customers achieve business value.

You can assemble this information into a Value Matrix™.

Building Your Value Matrix

To develop a Value Matrix, start with the roles involved in a typical purchase decision. Then add the high-level business objectives that they want to accomplish.

For example, an infection control solution might have the following stakeholders involved in a typical purchase decision:

- COO   • Value analysis committee   • Financial analyst   • VP of supply chain

- OR director   • Director of materials management   • Sterile processing department

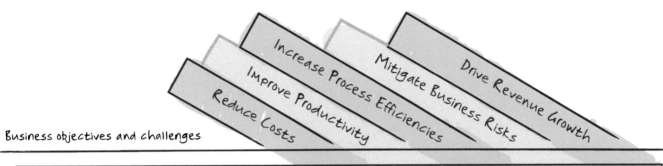

Business objectives and challenges

CLOSE Messaging

	Reduce Costs	Improve Productivity	Increase Process Efficiencies	Mitigate Business Risks	Drive Revenue Growth
Challenge Name Relevant Roles What does this look like now? Did you know?					
Loss What is this costing you?					
Opportunity What if...?					
Solution We can help... What you can save...					
Evidence We have achieved this already for...					

Here's what the Value Matrix looks like. You can use this to help organize your own value messaging.

Document the **Challenges** that prevent the prospect from meeting each business objective. Determine the key industry insights, so you can communicate the scope, cost and importance of the challenge. A typical challenge might be as follows:

> ## Challenge: Reducing the rate of surgical site infections
> ## Did you know ...
>
> • One in 25 patients acquire an infection in the hospital.
>
> • 20% of those are surgical site infections (SSIs).
>
> • Between 500,000 and 750,000 SSIs occur annually (hospitalsafetyscore.org).

Review each challenge against the roles to be sure that you document each role's unique challenges and value perspectives. This role mapping helps marketing, sales reps and channel partners easily determine which messaging is appropriate for each role.

Next, document the **Losses** that prospects experience as a result of not addressing these challenges (i.e. the cost of doing nothing).

Continuing with our infection control example:

> ## Loss
>
> • Each SSI incident costs $22,000 to $44,000 (hospitalsafetyscore.org).
>
> • The losses are estimated to be $17.6 million per year for a typical 50,000 patients-per-year hospital.

Next, following the CLOSE messaging methodology, each challenge corresponds with an **Opportunity** for improvement. Include the opportunities in your Value Matrix to paint a picture of what is possible.

> ## Opportunity: What if you could? ...
>
> • Improve sterilization quality.
>
> • Have fewer non-compliant instruments rejected and "dirty" complaints.
>
> • Reduce instrument handling.

As we move through the messaging, we document the specific **Solution**, highlighting the differentiating features of the products or services and quantifying how these features drive tangible business benefits. For example:

> **Solution**
>
> - Our infection control solution provides unique process improvements, automated pre-cleaning and low-flow / high-pressure cleaning.
> - This has been found to reduce the number of surgeries where site infections occur by 20%.
> - This can result in a potential savings of $3.52 million for a typical 50,000 patients-per-year hospital.

In addition to documenting a typical Loss and Solution value, also include a value calculator for each Challenge. It should calculate the "do nothing" costs for the Loss, as well as the tangible benefits derived from your proposed solutions. The calculators provide unique quantification of each of your prospect's challenges and opportunities.

Finally, correlate **Evidence** to verify how others have used your proposed solutions to obtain similar benefits and overcome the specific challenge. The evidence section lists relevant case studies, success stories and proof points. You can use case studies and "voice of the customer" testimonials from your website, press releases and analyst reports.

The Evidence is usually indexed. It presents evidence that matches the specific prospect – based on industry, location or size – as closely as possible.

To complete the matrix, detail the CLOSE messaging for each Challenge.

If some of your solutions are industry-specific, you can develop a separate matrix that's customized by vertical.

WHAT SHOULD A VALUE MATRIX LOOK LIKE?

This Value Matrix, created for Adaptive Insights, provides a framework to help sales reps and channel partners better communicate and quantify unique value to each prospect.

The Challenge: How to unlock finance productivity and enable your organization to be more strategic

Challenge
Did you know...
What it looks like now?...

It is an exciting time to be in finance.

• 3 out of 4 CFOs have seen their strategic influence increase over the last three years (Accenture).

• 75% see a change in fundamental strategy or structure over the coming year that they will influence (Accenture).

• Finance organizations are increasingly setting strategy and analyzing performance.

Is this what you are seeing in your own organization?

In speaking with other companies like yours, we see that many finance teams are excited about the potential, but are struggling to make this shift.

For example:

• Many core finance and accounting processes are manual, 75% of the effort in planning, reporting, analysis, and consolidation is wasted re-keying and manually rolling up data (Ventana).

• Worse 90% of spreadsheets contain data and formula errors, while 90% of users are convinced they are error free – creating substantial material risk as the pace of business accelerates (ACCA).

• In fact 64% of finance organizations report that their annual plans are out of date by the beginning of the fiscal year (Beyond Budgeting Round Table).

Loss
What this is costing you? ...

You too may be facing similar challenges, and if you are, your organization is likely spending way too much time and resources on the tactical parts of the finance process - collecting and rolling up data, checking for errors, copy and pasting – and without the tools to enable you to focus on business strategy and analysis.

It's hurting your finance team, and your company, because organizations that don't use analytics at the center of their business are less productive and less profitable than their peers that do – and grow at half the rate according to McKinsey.

Opportunity
What if...

What if you could....

• Plan and analyze in a fraction of the time it takes now?

• Access data you could trust at your fingertips?

• Move from managing the planning process to analyzing the plan?

• Reallocate resources from tactics to strategy?

Solution
We can help... What you can save ...

At Adaptive, we can help by providing a complete cloud planning, consolidation, reporting and analysis suite, enabling you to:

• Cut your time spent on manual processes and spreadsheets by 70%- with automated roll ups, centralized calculations, and workflow.

• Update plans, models, and forecasts quickly and reliably, with an easy to use centralized engine.

• Instantly see and analyze actuals, plans, and forecasts from anywhere - always based on the latest trusted data and consistent metrics.

• Improve forecast accuracy and analysis by enabling continual measurement between actuals and forecasts.

Evidence
We have achieved this already for...

For example, we have helped companies similar to yours achieve substantial savings, risk reduction and business value:

• Mfg: Konica Minolta reduced their budget process by 33% with Adaptive.

• Bus Svc: CORT Business Services cut their forecasting time by 80%.

• Health: Gentiva is saving about $500K a year using Adaptive versus their old on-premise system.

• Higher Ed: Montclair State achieved 211% ROI by cutting manual effort from their planning process.

• Software: Docusign cut time in spreadsheets from 80% to 20%.

• Financial Services: NorthStar cut reporting by more than 70%.

Sales sees Marketing's claims as boisterous

100

Marketing sees Sales as being too conservative

Developing Your Value Messaging: The Right Team and Process

You can use the Value Matrix as a framework to guide your creative process and help you fill in the blanks.

Assemble a team to collaborate on your value messaging. This team should include:

1. **Product marketing** to provide subject matter expertise around the industry research and product benefits.

2. **Marketing** to determine how your value messaging can be used throughout your content and campaigns.

3. **Sales**, including key reps and executives who have direct experience in articulating value to clients. This may include field and inside sales leadership.

4. **Sales enablement** to help determine how to put the value content into the tools that sales reps use every day.

5. **Sales training** to provide input on the challenges in learning, retention and adoption. These team members can help you decide how to best use your value content in sales training.

It's vital to include both sales and marketing when you develop your value messaging. They have different perspectives on value, both of which are needed to effectively communicate with customers.

Marketing often has great content about the value of your solution. However, sales may see marketing's claims as too boisterous and aggressive. Meanwhile, marketing often sees sales as too conservative and not as eloquent. Both must come to consensus on your value messaging.

After you assemble your value messaging team, start by looking at your prospects' key roles. Determine the top business objectives for each role. Use the Value Map categories of lowering costs, improving productivity, increasing process efficiencies, mitigating business risks and driving revenue growth. Discuss the challenges of achieving each objective. Then, add these challenges to your Value Matrix, adding more columns if needed.

Continue filling in the CLOSE boxes in your Value Matrix. At times, you may not have all the information. This is okay. Your Value Matrix will evolve over time, with the initial matrix helping you identify gaps and guide your content development.

You should also update your insights, case studies and other content on an annual basis to keep your campaigns and conversations fresh.

Applying the Value Matrix to Develop Better Marketing Content

The Value Matrix provides marketing with guidance on the best insights and value-focused content to use for different campaigns.

As a marketer, you can use each Challenge to fuel a specific provocative campaign – typically using each Challenge as a separate campaign message, with the CLOSE messaging providing the content for the campaign. You can also use the role index to target campaigns towards specific prospects.

Marketing can use the Value Matrix to help:

1. **Improve white papers and other marketing collateral,** focusing on buyer challenges, provocative insights and associated value messaging.

2. **Use prospect roles, objectives and challenges to customize content.** Marketing can serve challenge insights, solution recommendations and value based on content from your Value Matrix.

3. **Develop email campaigns around each challenge.** This will improve their nurturing efforts and give inside sales more effective content.

Since sales will also use the same framework, marketing and sales will have more effective and aligned messaging. This will help you seamlessly nurture customers and guide them through their decision-making journeys.

Applying the Value Matrix to Your Sales Conversations

Sales can use the Value Matrix to diagnose the prospect's challenges and then determine the appropriate CLOSE messaging. To use the Value Matrix, your sales reps and channels partners will ask each prospect a few key questions.

These discovery questions might include:

> **What is your role in the business?**
>
> Based on the role, you'll have ideas of what business objectives and challenges are the most relevant.

> **What is your business' vertical industry?**
>
> You can then select the most appropriate success stories that provide the most relevant evidence.

> **What are your business objectives?**
>
> For example, revenue growth, expense control, etc.

> **What are your challenges in meeting these objectives?**
>
> Based on the challenges, you'll have a complete dialogue of CLOSE messaging to use in your conversations and apply to your messaging.

> **Where are you in your decision-making process?**
>
> For example, ideas, exploration, evaluation, or selection.

The most appropriate CLOSE messaging can be used as "conversation fuel" for the following:

1. Outreach emails that contain provocative, challenge-focused content that is more effective than that in traditional emails

2. In-person conversations

3. Presentations to help guide the conversation

4. Interactive sales tools that provide value messaging, storytelling, insights and justification

When sales reps and channel partners use the Value Matrix with prospects, they should leverage the content. However, they should also make the conversation interactive versus just "spitting back" the CLOSE script. They can ask buyers questions during the conversation, such as:

• **Challenge and Loss**

Does this research and do these insights match your own experiences?

These are the challenges that we're seeing with others like you. But what are your challenges?

What are these issues costing you?

• **Opportunity**

Does this match the vision you had for a potential solution?

What additional elements did you have in mind?

• **Solution**

What legacy solutions do you have that are not meeting your needs?

Does the solution match what you were expecting?

Are you considering other providers? If so, what do you like or dislike about their solutions?

• **Evidence**

Which of these companies that we have worked with is the most similar to your own business?

What additional information would make you more comfortable that the business benefits are real and achievable for you?

The CLOSE Methodology can provide "conversation fuel" for the following interactions:

Email

Conversations

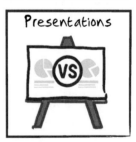

Presentations

Sales Tools

WHAT ARE THE BEST PRACTICES IN VALUE MESSAGING FOR SALES?

Jim Ninivaggi – Service Director, Sales Enablement Strategies, SiriusDecisions

Value is in the eye of the beholder, and each buyer has a unique "point of value."

First, it's critical to guide sales reps so they can understand and teach the buyer about important challenges. We need to give sales reps the right discovery questions to ask and the right content. This will help them discuss the prospect's challenges and the value the prospect can derive from overcoming these challenges.

Second, we must fuel the conversation, providing unique "soundbites" and dialogue for each challenge. For example, what is the research around the challenge? What is the cost of sticking with the status quo? What is the value of change if a prospect implements your proposed solution? What evidence do you have that similar customers have achieved business value from your solution?

Unfortunately, most content is one-size-fits-all. It includes endless PowerPoint decks that are about the company or product. It's not about the buyer's challenges and doesn't contain enough valuable insights.

The messaging must be challenge-centric, not product-centric. It should start with specific buyer challenges around high costs, lost productivity, process inefficiencies, business risks and revenue growth constraints. From there, you can talk about potential solutions and benefits, but you have to start your messaging around the challenges first.

One approach is the CLOSE storytelling method. Start by talking about Challenges, and then quantify the potential Loss, Opportunity, Solution and Evidence. CLOSE effectively articulates – in a systematic and buyer-centric way – how you can help the prospect overcome each challenge to achieve real business value.

This must be dynamic and agile. Sales must change the discovery questions and value messaging to connect with what the buyer cares about most. It is frustrating for prospects to spend time with a sales rep answering questions, only to be given a canned one-size-fits-all presentation in the end.

Your sales reps must connect the dots to value, and you can't do this with PowerPoint.

The challenge becomes the fuel. You need a messaging framework, commercial insights, financial justification and evidence to support and "fuel" your sales conversations.

Value Marketing

Value Marketing Tools

Today's marketers are producing never-ending streams of content to gain buyers' attention and nurture opportunities. More white papers ... more blog posts ... more lead-nurturing emails. In fact, **B2B marketers are spending 30% of their marketing budget on content marketing.**

However, SiriusDecisions found that **60-70% of the content produced by marketing goes unused.**

This is because more doesn't equal better.

As Ann Handley, Head of Content at MarketingProfs says, "We don't need more content. We need better content."

When you add value tools to your marketing mix, you can engage more prospects and turn them into customers. IDC research has shown that value marketing can generate **30% incremental response rates,** compared with traditional white paper campaigns with a **5% better conversion from leads to deals.** A typical value marketing campaign can generate **$1.5 million more revenue** than a traditional more product-centric campaign.

We don't need more content.

We need better content.

Optimize Your Content Marketing by Facilitating the Buyer's Journey

Content marketing is a big investment. According to a study by the Content Marketing Institute and MarketingProfs, it consumes 28% of total market-ing budgets annually. This already significant spending is increasing, as **55% of respondents plan to spend more on content over the next 12 months.**

However, even though budgets are significant and growing, marketers have serious doubts about the returns on these investments. **Only 41% have indicated that their content marketing efforts are effective.**

Content Marketing: Crisis of Confidence

According to the study, respondents indicated mixed sentiment on the effectiveness of go-to content like videos (40% ineffective rating), white papers, case studies and research reports (42% ineffective). Events seem to gather the highest effectiveness rankings, likely due to their more personalized and interactive nature. Newer techniques like microsites, ebooks and e-newsletters raise the most effectiveness doubts. Overall, you would think that with so much being spent on content marketing – and so much content being produced – the results would be higher.

One reason for the doubts is that content effectiveness is not measured by how it helps facilitate sales and generates revenue. Instead, most marketers measure how much content is produced and how many channels it is distributed on. This is "success by the pound". As content proliferates, relevancy to buyers is often lost in the mix. This means that the sheer volume of content overwhelms buyers.

Due to their personalized and interactive nature, Events gather the highest effectiveness rankings.

Relevancy is a Requirement

According to IDG Connect's "IT Buyer Survey", current content marketing strategies are producing **too much ineffective content that isn't relevant to buyers.** This lack of relevancy has a significant cost, including:

• Driving up content creation costs.

• Increasing the buyer's decision-making process by two weeks or more.

• Reducing your chances of making the buyer's selection shortlist by one third.

• Shrinking the chance of getting the sale by almost 50%.

Making your content more relevant can have a huge impact on your effectiveness and drive tangible ROI to your business. In fact, **86% of respondents cited that relevant content drove the buyer's decision.**

Can you develop a strategy to make your content more relevant, so it ultimately drives sales?

Achieve Relevancy by Mapping Content to the Buyer's Journey

One way to achieve relevancy is to align your content to each stage in the buyer's journey, facilitating the change management process that buyers must go through with multiple stakeholders in their organization.

According to IDC, the buyer's journey consists of the following steps:

1. **Ideas**   2. **Exploration**   3. **Evaluation**   4. **Selection**

In the Ideas phase, buyers need to achieve awareness that they have an issue. The, they prioritize the issue compared to other pains they are experiencing, and loosen the status quo so they can prepare for change. Helping the buyer diagnose and prioritize their issue, and quantifying the cost of "do nothing" is key.

Once buyers have committed to a change, they move to the Exploration and Evaluation phases. In these phases, buyers explore potential solutions and commit to a solution set (but not necessarily to a single provider). They must justify this solution set, especially in today's frugal times. This gives stakeholders a quantification of key financial indicators that signal the project is worthy of investment. These indicators include bottom-line impacts, investment requirements and ROI calculations.

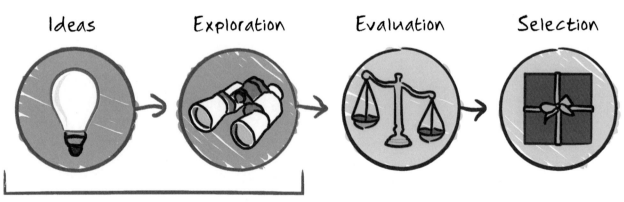

74% of deals are won
by the solution provider that helps set
the buying agenda (Forrester)

Once the solution is justified, the buyer choses a provider in the Selection phase. Since buyers are frugal and many committees are involved in the purchase process, a low price is often a key factor. However, the solution with the lowest purchase price may not deliver the lowest TCO. It also may have risks or may not deliver all of its expected benefits. In the final Selection phase, buyers should select the solution with the lowest overall TCO and best overall value. You must provide evidence, emotion and proof points to assure buyers that they are making the right decision.

For a marketer, the buyer's journey is an opportunity to provide content and tools that help buyers overcome resistance and drive their decision making. This means providing specific content to where each buyer is in the sales cycle.

Sales enablement must deliver content and tools that engage prospects each step of the way, especially early in the sales cycle when sales professionals aren't yet invited into the decision-making process.

When content has a specific purpose and facilitates each step in the buyer's journey, you can significantly reduce the amount of content you need to drive sales. Plus, you'll improve the effectiveness of your marketing.

Content Investments Are Effective When Aligned With the Buyer's Journey

Marketers are investing a substantial portion of their budget in content. Research from the Content Marketing Institute and MarketingProfs indicates that content currently consumes **28% of marketing budgets** on average. According to their study of over 5,000 B2B marketers, **55% of respondents plan to increase this spending over the next year.**

These large investments show the important role content plays in the marketing mix to fuel decision making.

However, marketers indicate that even with substantial and increased content budgets, their number-one challenge remains **producing the right type of content that effectively engages prospects and customers (54%).**

55% of marketers plan to increase spending to create new content next year.

65% of this content goes unused as marketers fail to produce content that effectively engages prospects.

And the challenges don't end there. Results indicate a continued and decided crisis in confidence with content marketing. Close to half of marketers indicated that some of the most popular tactics aren't effective, including microsites (54%) and eBooks (55%). The good news is that some tactics are perceived worthy, including tactics that involve direct interaction with buyers such as in-person events (69% effective) and webinars / webcasts (64%). More personalized and relevant content also ranked as more effective, including the use of blogs (60%), case studies (58%) and videos (60%).

Is this lack of effectiveness due to the newness of content marketing compared to more traditional ways to engage buyers? Is it due to the challenges of producing enough relevant and compelling content? Does it relate to a lack of measurement and proof points that prospects are using the content? Is it because the content fails to impact purchase decisions? Is it because today's buyers are more empowered, skeptical and frugal than ever before? The research didn't answer these questions but did highlight the characteristics of top performers.

The results indicate that best-in-class marketers document their content marketing strategies (54% of top-performers vs. 35% on average), invest more in content (37% vs. 28%) and place a higher importance on engagement as the end goal (89% vs. 81%).

EFFECTIVENESS RATINGS OF B2B TACTICS

	Tactic
69%	In-Person Events
64%	Webinars/Webcasts
60%	Videos
60%	Blogs
58%	Case Studies
58%	White Papers
58%	Research Reports
58%	eNewsletters
55%	eBooks
54%	Microsites

THE CONTENT MARKETING — BUYER DISCONNECT

Dan Sixsmith, VP, Value Consultant at Alinean

According to a newly published report, there is a serious disconnect between the content that B2B buyers expect from marketers, and what is actually being produced and delivered. In the new study from The Economist Group , 93% of B2B marketers are incorrectly connecting their content to a product or service. Translation: a sales pitch.

Unfortunately, most marketing is not what buyer's expect - value focused and personalized. Instead, the majority of content marketing is being perceived as one-size-fits-all messaging which is inwardly focused-on the vendors company, team, history, awards, products, features, functions.

The good news: B2B execs still seek out help from solution providers to solve their complex issues and often turn to online content for critical challenge-focused information. The bad news: they are having trouble finding the content they need.

So how do marketers better align their content marketing to what prospective buyers want? A few thoughts to chew on:

It's Not One and Done: A piece of content should not be viewed as a one and done proposition by marketers.

The reality is that it typically takes 9 touches just to connect with the prospect, and consumption of 12 pieces of content before a prospect is ready to speak to sales. Your content marketing should be about building a lasting relationship with the prospect, versus trying to close the deal on the first date. You have amassed a treasure trove of valuable content. Delivering the right content to the buyer at the right point in the customer journey is key. View your content much as a publisher would - as a step on the way to deeper connections with your audience.

It's Not Me, It's You: Content is best when it focuses on the addressable business challenges you can help the buyer solve, and the business benefits that can be achieved. Prospects favor content that is not a company / product pitch, but focuses on their challenges and positive outcomes, Even though you have every right to be proud of what you market and sell, buyers don't really care about that. Instead, they care about themselves – the pains they are living and how you can help them. Guy Kawasaki, the former Mac evangelist and current thought leader declared," Show people how you will make history together. Sell the dream (of a better future), not a product."

The 5S's of Content Marketing - Marketing used to be about the 4P's (Product, Place, Promotion and Price), now it should be more about the 5S's: storytelling, substance, speed, simplicity and science. Powerful content needs all of these components.

Storytelling

A primitive part of our brains connects with stories, as if we are still sitting around the fire recanting stories of a good hunt or harvest. The story should reflect the essence of the brand and be leveraged to create personalized customer experiences that last beyond the sale and deliver long-term relationships. Everyone loves a story where a hero tangles with and finally defeats a villain. Introduce the antagonist. What is the current challenge out there that needs solving? Describe the pain the prospect is feeling, the magnitude and cause of this problem and then prescribe a cure. How did you save the day? Make it exciting. The brain doesn't pay attention to boring things, according to scientist John Medina.

Substance

The messaging needs align with a buyer challenge, an issue that the marketplace and buyer needs resolved. In some cases, this challenge might be hidden, and the typical buyer might not even know how serious it is. Explain the 'why' before the 'how.' Original content backed by research scores best with audiences. Establish authority and subject matter expertise. A solution in search of a problem carries far less appeal. Customers don't buy products or services, they first buy into solving a significant, priority challenge.

Speed

It is 'short attention span theatre' out there. You have 8 seconds to get and keep a buyers attention so your content needs to get to the point as to what challenges should be addressed and how you will help solve their woes. Content should be fast-paced and loaded with excitement. Think simple visuals, contrast and the Elevator Pitch.

Simplicity

The task of leaders is to simplify. Tell the prospect how you will make her life better, the expected value— not about your feeds and speeds. And do it concisely. Create content about the challenges, loss, opportunity, solution and evidence that can fit on the "back of a napkin."

Science

Leverage data you have collected about your prospects to create relevant content across all customer touch points. Where is the prospect on his decision journey? What flavor of content should you offer? What do you know about them that can help customize the content to their industry, role and challenges?

The Bottom-Line

There is a tremendous opportunity for marketers to align their content to what today's buyer expects — personalized and value-focused — and more effectively connect and engage prospective clients to drive more demand and incremental revenue. The keys? Take a longer-term view of content, center it around business challenges, and leverage the 5S's of content marketing to drive more wins.

Facilitating the Buyer's Journey

Different marketing content and tools can facilitate buyers' decisions throughout their journey. Your content can also help sales better engage buyers during each stage of the sales cycle and close more deals. The more aligned your tools are with each stage in the buyer's journey, the better you will engage prospects.

For today's more conservative buyer, it's often easier to do nothing than to change, because change comes with costs and risks. In the beginning of the buyer's journey, you can use provocative insights, interactive benchmarks and diagnostic tools to help buyers confirm and prioritize their issues. These tools can also help buyers uncover issues they might not know they have. The insight from these benchmarks and diagnostic tools can help buyers realize that addressing a specific issue is a priority and that it's vital to change from the status quo.

Later in the buyer's journey, economic-focused executives demand that every investment deliver a bottom-line impact, positive ROI and a quick payback. Marketers must prove the solution's value to frugal buyers, effectively communicating and quantifying the potential savings and incremental benefits. It's vital to show that the solution delivers the highest value at the lowest cost.

One-size-fits-all content doesn't work. Buyers now expect content to speak to their specific needs and challenges. You must personalize your value messaging, insights, benchmarks, diagnoses, benefits and business case. This is especially true, because more stakeholders are involved in the decision-making process and each requires content that is personalized to their particular challenges and value perspectives.

Content marketing is a significant investment, yet most marketers have little faith that their current content marketing strategies are effective. Marketers often measure content marketing success "by the pound." However, buyers suffer from information overload and only want the right information at the right time.

Marketers who map content to the buyer's journey can reduce the amount of content they produce to just what is needed to facilitate purchase decisions. This enables buyers to make quicker decisions. It also allows sales to use content to engage earlier and more effectively.

The latest interactive content – such as dynamic benchmarks, diagnostic assessments and calculators – can improve your ability to engage today's more empowered, skeptical and frugal buyers.

The following is a recommendation for specific value-focused and more personalized content to address the buyers' needs at each step in their journey:

	Discovery	Consideration	Decision
Buyer Needs	Investigate and prioritize the issue(s) as one(s) to be addressed Loosening of the status quo Committing to change	Exploring possible solutions Committing to a solution set Justifying the decision	Making the right product / service selection Assuring that the selected solution represents best value
Recommended Content	Value Storytelling Interactive White Papers Provocative Webcasts and Events Diagnostic Assessment Tools	Solution Case Studies Video Testimonials Solution Oriented White Papers Interactive ROI / Business Case Tools	Feature / Function Comparisons TCO White Papers TCO Comparison Tools

THE BUYER'S JOURNEY OR HIDE AND SEEK?

Dan Sixsmith, VP, Value Consultant an Alinean

Once upon a time a few decades ago, selling was simpler. Picture the NYC garment district in its heyday, the late 80s. My colleagues and I would stand outside the buildings where our clients and prospects worked. When they came out for lunch or a meeting: "Bingo!" It was show time! We'd pitch them as they walked or nab them for a lunch presentation.

We were in control of the supply and the sales cycle. The "buyer's journey" was from 37th and 6th to 40th and 5th (or as many blocks as it took to make our pitch and gain a commitment).

Things have changed a bit since then, for the garment industry as well as how we sell.

Technology has made it easier to market and sell your products, but at the same time, gaining and maintaining buyer interest has grown increasingly difficult.

Today's buyer's journey is more of a game of hide-and-seek than a linear process. Your prospects are appearing, consuming content, engaging and then disappearing.

And this is not a one-on-one game. The average deal has over eight decision makers, a 43% increase from three years ago (IDC). Each stakeholder has a different spot at which they join the decision-making process, so while some may be well on their way to selecting a solution, others are just making up their minds that they have a problem worth addressing.

This new game is a tough one, as:

• A whopping 58% of B2B deals stall as the buyer goes dark, leaving sales scratching their heads as to what happened (SBI).

• Deals that do close are taking 24% longer to do so compared to just two years ago (SiriusDecisions).

• Only 59% of sales reps achieved their quota in 2014, down sharply from 67% in 2013 (Accenture).

But maybe your deal is not stalling and the prospect didn't go dark. Perhaps one of the many decision makers is just getting started, heavily researching the opportunity and potential solutions. Maybe you just missed your prospect on another channel. While they disappeared off email, they may be very active on social or mobile.

Business buyers who appear to be hiding may actually be quite active. They might be conducting further research on you and your competitors' websites, actively seeking advice in social communities, and conversing with analysts and peers about their plans.

Marketers need to be everywhere, engaging prospects with personalized content to facilitate the buying process long after the initial interest is generated. And sales must quickly pick up the conversation with decision makers who are at different stages in the buying journey and have unique perspectives on value and what your solution can do for them.

So how do you succeed in this rapidly changing playing field? Here's a start:

Engage Early and Often

The Holy Grail of engagement is delivering the right content to the right prospect at the right time in the right channel. Easier said than done.

Connect all the dots, leverage technology and be ready to engage at every touch point. Focus on the challenges your product solves, not on your features and functions. Hire a Chief Content Officer or equivalent and build out a wealth of meaningful content. Arm your sales reps with this content so they can fuel provocative and effective conversations. Use data to inform your team about prospect behavior and adjust your messaging according to their role in the organization and stage in the journey. This will involve a good deal of trial and error. Rinse and repeat.

Personalize Your Content and Focus on Your Value

If you provide the wrong content, your buyers will go dark for good. A recent study in The Economist indicates that 71% of buyers disengaged with a vendor because their content and sales meetings were all about pitching products and not about facilitating the buyer journey and showing value. Since each opportunity is unique and each decision maker has a different value perspective, what value means to each opportunity and stakeholder is quite different. As a result, a one-size-fits-all approach won't work.

Your content must be interactive, visual, and personal. At Alinean, we have addressed this issue through the creation of a platform that intelligently delivers content tailored to the prospect's industry, role, company size, challenges, business goals and KPIs. The result is higher-value leads to sales, greater engagement, more provocative conversions, fewer stalls and more closed deals.

Here are some key takeaways from our experience:

1. Serve up content in an entertaining fashion to emotionally connect with buyers and stimulate the decision-making process. Tell a story about your value and paint a clear picture to contrast "business as usual" versus your improvement plan.

2. Deliver insights and financial justification. Help buyers diagnose and uncover priority issues, quantify benefits and prove ROI. Capture discovery data, value plans and realized results. Use these new insights and get smarter from each engagement.

3. Gain credibility and provide proof of value via success stories and "voice of the customer" videos.

Sales as Marketers: Sales Reps Can No Longer Just Sell

The huge spike in inbox-cluttering marketing messages and unwanted sales pitches has further strained the trust factor between prospective buyers and salespeople. Therefore, sales reps are now being called upon to establish greater credibility with clients. They can do so by using insights, storytelling, justification and content to become subject matter experts and thought leaders—a role typically handled by marketing.

Marketers as Sales: The Role of Marketing is Evolving

The complexity of the buyer's "decision space", as put by Epsilon's CEO Andy Frawley in his excellent book, Igniting Customer Connections, now requires organizations to connect with buyers both virtually and directly. Organizations must use impactful and personalized content to meet a prospect wherever they turn up and then guide them to the eventual finish line. Therefore, marketers are now responsible for nurturing not just the top-of-funnel leads, but engaging them throughout the decision-making process. Marketers are also responsible for revenue growth, increasing numbers and carrying quotas. Sounds like selling to me.

Employees as Publishers: Everyone Needs a Personal Brand and a Point of View

The more 'feet on the street' to engage buyers, the better. Buyers want to know what employees – not just the CEO or salespeople – think about your company and products. Encourage blogging and let the culture and true face of your organization come forward. This will help buyers evaluate what it will be like to do business with you.

With revenue growth at the core of all challenges in 2015 and beyond, the elusive buyer can be found in any number of channels.

The question is, are you ready to facilitate the buyer's journey for the new game of hide and seek? Tag, you're it!

Take a look at interactive white papers

The Value of Alinean

Iron Mountain Cost-Saving Advisor

ADP Human Capital Management Challenge

View these whitepapers at
FrugalnomicsSurvivalGuide.com/
resources

Evolving Beyond Traditional White Papers to Generate Demand

White papers have become the "crack cocaine" of marketing. Marketers are addicted to using them to attract interest and fuel marketing automation nurturing campaigns. As a result, prospects' inboxes are jammed with offers to download white papers.

With so many download offers, most white papers don't help companies stand out from the crowd. This is because your prospects think they are all the same – long, boring and focused on your company versus on them and their issues.

To engage today's "cold as ICE" buyers, you must:

1. Focus your white papers on your buyers' challenges to give an outside-in view from the prospect's perspective. Don't focus white papers on your solution, an inside-out perspective.

2. Personalize your white papers to address each prospect's unique challenges, what it's costing them to do nothing and the specific value of your solutions.

3. Use visual storytelling versus endless amounts of text.

Introducing Interactive White Papers

Interactivity is making white papers the "king of content" once again. It transforms one-size-fits-all, static white papers into personalized resources. Interactive white papers help buyers diagnose their issues, quantify the costs of doing nothing and see your unique value.

Used in place of static white papers, interactive white papers can fuel your marketing campaigns. They are web apps designed for prospects who don't have the time to read lengthy, boring white papers. Interactive white papers use discovery to fine-tune content, deliver a visual story and provide financial justification for your solution.

A prospect simply enters some basic profile information, and the app will return a fully customized online story and downloadable white paper. An ideal interactive white paper is:

1. Personalized to include the right challenges, opportunities, solution recommendations and case studies.

2. Concise, because content is filtered to only include what is most relevant to the buyer's role and needs.

3. Logical to appeal to buyers' Logos. It's rational to quantify the "cost of doing nothing" and the value of your proposed solutions.

4. Emotional to appeal to buyers' Pathos. It includes customized visual storytelling and video to stimulate the buyer's interest. It also contains buying triggers that align with the buyer's challenges and role in the decision-making process.

5. Credible to appeal to buyers' Ethos, providing visual success stories to gain trust.

Interactive white papers can help you overcome the challenges of traditional white papers, as they are value-focused, visual and relevant. IDC found that interactive white papers generate 3x more leads than traditional white papers, as well as 150% more qualified leads per white paper campaign.

Marketers are addicted to using white papers to attract interest. As a result, prospects' inboxes are jammed with them.

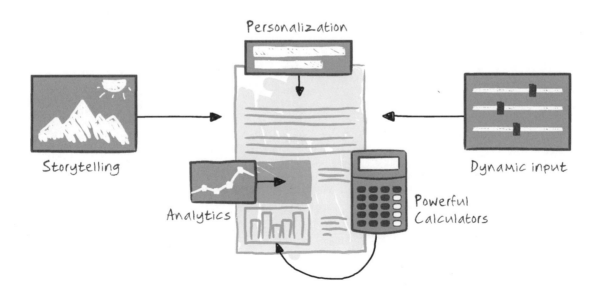

Anatomy of an Interactive White Paper

Personalization

Storytelling

Analytics

Powerful Calculators

Dynamic input

IT'S ONLY A MATTER OF TRUST

While the medium is important, buyers have also indicated that the source of the content matters.

In our research, buyers indicate that unbiased content from leaders in their industry is the most valuable. So, it's no surprise that the most valuable content is peer advice, recommendations and stories. Content from industry analysts – such as research and insights – also ranks as well trusted. This content helps illuminate opportunities so buyers can choose the best solution.

Although not a third-party source, content from consultants and vendors is also perceived as valuable. This is good news for marketers, as it represents a great opportunity to provide content and advice that helps facilitate buyer decisions.

Most Trusted Sources:

Peers
84%

Industry
Analysts
65%

Consultants
and Vendors
43%

Crafting Provocative Emails That Work

Most emails try to sell, sell, sell.

However, to engage prospects, you must stop selling and start helping.

Email marketing is vital to most demand generation programs. However, most email marketing falls short. It's often too long, too cookie-cutter or too heavily focused on a company's products.

Your prospects' inboxes are jammed with requests for meetings, demos and downloads. So, how do you stand out from the crowd and improve the effectiveness of your email marketing campaigns?

Here are five keys to crafting provocative emails that will help you better connect with prospects and motivate them to take action:

1. Open with a bang.

You only have a few seconds to capture a prospect's attention, so it's vital to set the right tone in your email's opening lines. Give prospects a reason to keep reading. Research from IDC found that buyers are always willing to engage with sales reps who can help them:

• Understand more about their industry landscape

• Gain insights on challenges they should address

• Learn about innovative strategies that have worked well at similar companies

• Detail and quantify specific revenue growth, competitive advantage or bottom line improvements that you can deliver

Your emails shouldn't sell but educate prospects and facilitate their purchase journey. You must convey one of these key messages in your email's opening to show prospects immediate value.

2. Be concise.

B2B buyers have more demands and distractions than ever. They don't have time to read long emails. Get to the point. Keep your emails short – no more than five sentences with each sentence in a line by itself. This will make it easy for your busy prospects to skim your content and find the key information that they need.

3. Tell your value story ... don't pitch your products.

Most prospecting emails talk about how great a product or service is. However, B2B buyers don't care about this, at least not yet. They care about their challenges and what you can do to help solve them.

Instead of selling, tell a story about your prospect's issue, what it's costing them and how you can solve it. Use the CLOSE storytelling framework that's outlined in the "Opportunities" chapter to shape your story.

4. Create different emails for different stages in the sales cycle.

The majority of your prospects aren't ready to buy, yet. They seek knowledge to guide their decision-making process. However, the majority of prospecting emails speak to customers who want to buy now. This means that B2B organizations are missing the opportunity to connect with early-stage leads and drive future sales.

Craft at least three types of prospecting emails – one for each stage of the buyer's journey. These emails should address the following topics:

• **Why change?** At this stage, your buyer isn't sure that they have a challenge worth addressing. Create emails that share the latest research on the issue and outline the cost of doing nothing.

• **Why now?** The buyer knows that they have an issue worth addressing but isn't sure if addressing it should be a priority. Contrast your solution with "business as usual" and legacy solutions. Quantify that your solution is low risk and can deliver quick ROI.

• **Why you?** At this stage, your buyer wants information about your solution. Don't blow it by inundating them with features and solution mumbo-jumbo. Your email should discuss the business reason why your solution is the best choice – with the lowest risk and highest reward.

5. Don't ask for too much.

Many prospecting emails ask for the prospect to do too much. Call a sales rep! Visit this web page! Download this resource! However, the less you ask for, the more you will gain.

Include one strong call to action in your emails. Your call to action should be a value-add offer with exclusive content, such as a personalized interactive white paper, benchmark report or diagnostic assessment. Think consultative when it comes to content you promote in your calls to action. Also be sure to minimize distractions by only asking your prospects to click one link or view one attached file.

If you want prospects to schedule a call or meeting with you, suggest a specific time. If you leave it vague, you won't get as many responses.

Be Provocative Without Being Arrogant - Diagnostic Assessments

One key to getting early attention from buyers is to be provocative – gain the buyer's attention with key statistics and challenges. Basically, try to rock their world.

However, it's sometimes tough to take a provocative stance without being perceived as assumptive or pushy.

So, how can you proactively engage buyers without being perceived as confrontational or arrogant?

There are several ways to accomplish this, but one of the best is to deliver compelling insights via a diagnostic assessment tool. This tool is a self-service, interactive survey that prospects can access from your website to gain insight into their top business challenges.

The diagnostic assessment starts by asking your prospects a few discovery questions – no more than 10 – about their current practices and spending.

You run the risk of overwhelming your prospect when you include too many calls to action.

BUYING BY COMMITTEE: NURTURING FOR SUCCESS

Brian Hession, CEO / founder of Oceanos

Value marketing and selling success requires identifying the buying committee and then nurturing them with the appropriate value messaging. The goal is to educate the buying committee on how your product or solution helps to minimize risk, increase efficiencies, and directly impact the bottom line.

The first step is to determine the individuals that comprise the committee. Start by casting a wide net to find all potential contacts across functions and departments. To make this easier, consider mapping within three groups: Decision Makers, Influencers, and End-Users. Each company differs in structure and those elusive champions you need could fall within any of these categories.

To ascertain the actual names and resulting contact information, you can research social media and purchase a list. To scale this approach, partner with a firm that can identify these contacts and provide you with account and contact level intelligence to assist in scoring and prioritization.

If the buying cycle is 12-18 months, then it is likely that the composition of the buying committee will change. There will be attrition, new hires, promotions, and lateral moves with which to contend. Some of this information will be uncovered during the normal sales process, but the faster you learn of these changes, the better. This requires a workflow that ensures that your contact and business intelligence is up-to-date and complete. To increase success, leverage a data advisory firm and you will be a more confident value marketing and selling expert.

Brian Hession

Then, it scores their responses and delivers unique, data-driven insights. The insights are based on the prospect's responses, as well as comparisons to your proprietary database of best practices and benchmarks.

The diagnostic assessment answers the following questions:

• Which of your prospect's practices are good? Which are less than stellar?

• What is your prospect overlooking?

• Where is your prospect spending more or less than the competition?

• Is your prospect ahead of the competition or falling behind?

As more prospects and sales reps use the diagnostic assessment tool, your scoring and benchmark database will grow. It will automatically update your data, so you can deliver real-time insights.

These benchmarks aren't generic research – that may or may not apply to your prospect's challenges – but a way for you to deliver consultative and data-driven insights.

Once the issues are uncovered, the diagnostic assessment tool can go further to:

• Highlight the highest priority areas of concern

• Estimate the current cost of doing nothing

• Recommend potential solutions and next steps to help resolve the top-priority issues

• Provide an estimate of how these solutions might reduce costs and risks while driving business value

Take a look at diagnostic assessment tools:

UpToDate Clinical Decisions Support ROI Calculator

CenturyLink Colocation ROI Calculator

I Want My ROI - Portal of different generic calculators

View these tools at
FrugalnomicsSurvivalGuide.com/ resources

ARE THE 4 P'S STILL RELEVANT OR IN NEED OF A MAJOR RESET?

If you've taken a marketing course over the past few decades, you were likely schooled on the 4 P's: Product, Place, Promotion and Price.

Developed in the early 60s by the marketer E. Jerome McCarthy and popularized by Philip Kotler, the four P's have maintained a prominent role in how marketers develop go-to-market strategies and set their "marketing mix" – a recipe for balancing the ingredients of revenue success.

For B2B solution providers, the 4 P's include:

• **Product** – How your product or service fits into the adoption life cycle (innovation, early adopter, early/late majority and laggards). Marketers must also understand the product mix - increasing the depth of their features and potentially the number of product or service lines.

• **Place** – Where you can purchase the product or service, such as directly from a sales rep, through a channel partner, in a store or online.

• **Promotion** - Communication to provide prospects with information about your products or services. This includes advertising, public relations and content marketing. It also includes sales presentations, collateral and tools.

• **Price** - The amount a customer pays for the product or service. Pricing is based on the product's perceived value, competitive comparisons and price elasticity.

However, are these 4 P's still relevant? In a world that has changed so much over the past 55 years, they are likely not. Today's buyers are more empowered with:

1. Information. They rely on the Internet, social media and peer recommendations to make more informed purchase decisions.

2. More ways to buy.

3. Products that are personalized and customized for their needs.

Today's B2B buyers are also tougher to engage, as they have:

1. Shorter attention spans. The average attention span is now only eight seconds – less than that of a goldfish.

2. Buying committees that are more risk adverse and require more diligence in every decision to avoid making a mistake.

3. Intense economic focus. They care about the bottom-line impact, return on investment and fast payback.

B2B buyers want solution providers to focus on business outcomes and value – not price and push promotions.

As a result, research from Forrester has indicated that the 4 P's of marketing are outdated and in need of a major rethink. Forrester suggests a new set of P's for B2B that are focused on solving customer challenges and delivering value. These new 4 P's are Problem, Pattern, Path and Proof.

The move from the 4 P's of product/solution selling to the 4 P's of outcome / value marketing & selling include:

• **Problem** - What are the customer's business objectives and challenges that you are helping them to solve? Are they fully aware of these issues? How will you help them diagnose new challenges and prioritize those of which they are already aware? What is the cost of sticking with business as usual or the status quo?

• **Pattern** – Once the customer is aware that a problem exists and that it is a priority, how will your solution help them solve the problem? How will they use your product or service to overcome the challenges and derive value?

• **Path** - How will the solution be purchased? How can you help facilitate the complex decision cycle to gain consensus amongst the multiple stakeholders? What does the customer need to be successful?

• **Proof** - What is the quantified value that your solution will deliver with regards to reducing costs, driving incremental revenue/margin or other tangible business benefits? What additional business benefits will your solution deliver, such as reducing risks, or driving agility? How have others obtained similar value at low risk?

Although we shouldn't totally abandon time-honored frameworks, using the same marketing and selling practices of 50 years ago may not be the best approach today.

It might be time to evolve the traditional 4 P's to focus more on the buyer from the outside in, as opposed to the product from the inside out. Working on the 4 new P's of Problem, Pattern, Path and Proof may be what we need to shift to value-focused marketing and selling.

The 4 P's

Product focused	⟶	Buyer focused
① Product		① Problem
② Place		② Pattern
③ Promotion		③ Path
④ Price		④ Proof

Connect with Your Audience Via Webcasts, Podcasts, Audio and Videos

Even as transactions move online, people still prefer to buy from other people. Buyers feel a personal connection when they hear subject matter experts speak on a podcast or watch them in a video. These visual and aural formats are becoming a preferred form of content. They help you connect with executives early in the sales cycle and later build a business case.

Webcasts, podcasts and videos provide a dynamic platform for pundits, subject matter experts and satisfied customers to deliver key messages. They help buyers:

• Get ideas from thought leaders on what issues are important and how they should be prioritized.

• Gain the ammunition to challenge the status quo within the organization and help stakeholders understand that there is a "cost of doing nothing".

• Understand what solutions are available and how others have successfully used these solutions to drive tangible business outcomes.

• See the differences between potential solutions.

The best podcasts, videos and webcasts deliver content that facilitates a specific step in the buyer's journey.

Tracking usage of this content shows some dramatic differences in format preferences based on where prospects are in the buying journey. For example:

• Podcasts are popular at only the earliest stages in the buying cycle. Busy executives and travelers enjoy listening to podcasts while they are on the road. Podcasts are effective at providing research insights and education but they quickly fall off later in the decision cycle.

• Videos have the largest impact during the first half of the buyer's journey. They are used extensively during the discovery phase to educate stakeholders on opportunities. They are also used during the consideration phase to illuminate the business reasons for change, present case studies and provide solution overviews.

• Webcasts influence the entire sales cycle. They educate early-stage leads, help provide business justification and highlight success stories. They also give implementation advice and help buyers make decisions.

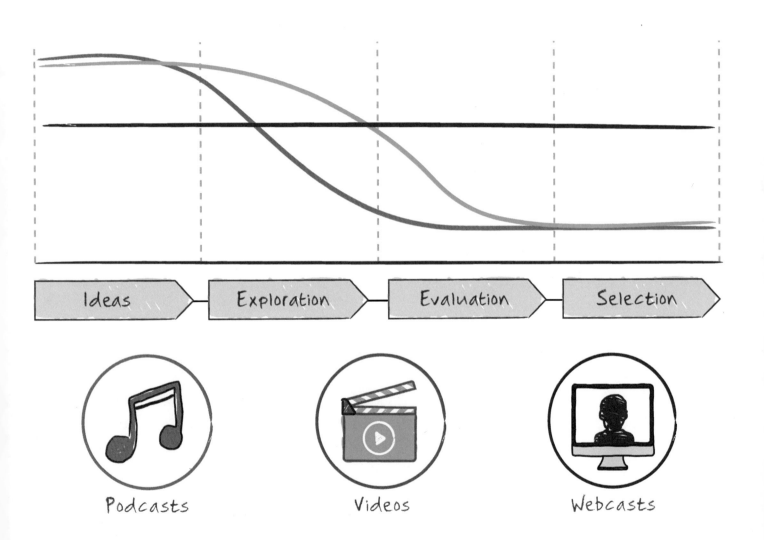

Effectiveness of marketing techniques over a buyers journey

Ideas > Exploration > Evaluation > Selection

Podcasts   Videos   Webcasts

Show Your Value With ROI Calculators

ROI calculators are self-service tools that prospects can use to quickly determine whether your solutions can provide them with tangible benefits, fast payback and substantial return on investment.

These calculators ask a few discovery questions to gain an idea of the prospect's business and opportunities from improvement. Using direct research or estimates, these tools simulate the impact of your solutions and quantify any potential benefits, costs and ROI.

Many calculators let prospects delve deeper and change all the assumptions and defaults. This gives them a more precise idea of the benefits they can achieve.

ROI calculators are valuable landing pages for direct marketing campaigns, as well as for educating and capturing leads. They deliver real, quantifiable results. For example, a major software vendor used an ROI calculator to:

• Achieve a 15% visit-to-sale conversion rate (versus 5% for regular registrants)

• Double its qualified leads, compared with all its other web promotions combined

• Increase length of stay by 340% (17 minutes for those who used the calculator versus 5 minutes for regular visitors)

• Increase average page views by 314% (22 page visits for those who used the calculator versus seven page visits for regular visitors)

Here's why the ROI calculator was successful:

• It was built by a credible third party, not the vendor.

• It included white papers and case studies from existing customers to back up all the benefit claims.

• Users could review and change all key assumptions until they were comfortable with the ROI results.

• It was part of a value-oriented campaign to attract an audience that cares about ROI and business value.

• Prospects could get results in just a few minutes. However, they could also go more in depth and fine-tune their results.

• Users could share reports with other stakeholders and decision makers.

ARE ROI CALCULATORS DEAD?

Many ROI calculators fall short. Here's a summary of their issues, along with how to improve your efforts to drive better demand generation and nurturing:

The Black Box

Many ROI calculators are too simple. They collect basic profile data and – with the press of a button – magically generate positive ROI results.

Although easy to use, these black box ROI calculators:

• Don't provide customized results to match the unique challenges and "points of value" that are important to each customer and their role in the decision process.

• Don't let customers review and edit key assumptions.

• Don't deliver the calculations that show customers how you are determining their value. This makes them skeptical that you can solve their problems.

Solution: Good ROI calculators allow prospects to review details and assumptions. They customize results to match specific profiles, buyer roles and business challenges. They also allow prospects to edit all assumptions and review the details of all calculations to gain buy-in.

Third-party development and delivery can provide credibility. Prospects are more likely to trust an independent third party's calculations than your own calculations.

Solution Agnostic

These ROI calculators are often simplified so much that they don't reflect the unique differentiators of your solution.

Solution: An effective ROI calculator will identify your unique differentiators and tie them to the prospect's value realization. Your tool should contain unique value calculations and documented impacts. It should also provide third-party research and success stories to prove that the savings are achievable.

Pain vs. Gain

Many ROI calculators jump too quickly to "justify the gain". However, at this early point in the buyer's journey, they should help prospects "quantify the pain". These tools should help prospects understand the cost and priority of the challenges before showing how your solution can deliver ROI.

Solution: Good ROI calculators provide diagnostic assessments to help prospects uncover issues and quantify their current costs of doing nothing BEFORE discussing solutions or quantifying benefits.

All About the Benjamins

Many ROI calculators focus too much on numbers and too little on value storytelling.

Solution: A good ROI calculator uses numbers to cement the value messaging. It combines emotional storytelling, evidence (e.g. success stories), rational justification and ROI calculations.

Value Selling: It's All About the Conversation

The key to getting more sales is improving the effectiveness of your customer conversations. Since you don't often meet customers face to face, this also means improving the conversations in your online meetings and proposals.

Your sales reps must evolve from pitching products to helping customers connect the dots between where they are now and where they want to go.

This means going beyond just a sales methodology – like Challenger, Insight or Spin Selling – to provide reps with all the elements they need to be successful: a combination of value messaging, customer-facing value sales tools, and value coaching.

Is Value Selling The Key to Social Selling Success?

B2B buyers are waiting longer to engage with sales reps. Meanwhile, the need for reps to engage buyers earlier has never been greater.

If you're able to connect with buyers earlier, you can gain a significant advantage over your competitors.

B2B buyers are using social media early in the purchase process to research their challenges and get recommendations from peers. Today's buyers use an average of five social channels during their purchase process . If you want to connect with today's "cold as ICE" buyers, you need to get social.

However, you can't use social media just to push your products or services. Buyers will only engage with you if you add value to their social streams.

Today's top sales performers are doing in-depth research on their buyers. They're providing value-add insights that help prospects identify and solve their key business challenges. This means going beyond just mining public data about your prospects and sending them information about your products and services.

Successful social selling helps buyers understand the potential costs, risks and lost opportunities of not addressing their key business or competitive challenges. You can use insights to educate buyers but you must deliver insights that are NOT publicly available.

So, where do these proprietary insights come from?

Sales reps often struggle to pull together all the content they need to be successful, making it important for marketing to play a key role in sales enablement. Marketing can create the best insights by helping to:

1. Define the most common challenges by role and industry.

2. Collect commercial insights (industry research) around each challenge. You can find these in published studies and survey responses.

3. Conduct proprietary research to determine the impact of these challenges and the value of potential solutions. Ask third-party researchers to gather unique insights across the market. You can use interactive tools to collect all of the insights that you gather from prospects.

4. Build a value-messaging matrix with the CLOSE content to fuel email and social prospecting, as well as in-person conversations. Teach sales reps how to use your value messaging to craft more compelling emails.

5. Create Point-of-View (POV) conversation guides or presentations to guide reps through more compelling meetings and conversations.

6. Develop interactive sales tools to guide reps on what to present in each selling situation. These guided selling tools can provide insights that are personalized for each prospect. Diagnostic assessments, benchmarks and personalized ROI calculations are all proven to be effective.

Value Selling Tools: Communicate Your Value, Quantify Your ROI and Stand Out from the Pack

Let's face it ... PowerPoint won't help you close deals.

A Zogby study found that more than **one third of buyers would rather visit their dentist than sit through another boring PowerPoint presentation.**

So, if your trusted PowerPoint decks aren't working, what is?

"Although organizations want sales reps to have value-centric conversations, they arm reps with endless amounts of product-focused materials," says Jim Ninivaggi, Practice Director for Sales Enablement, SiriusDecisions. "We need to move beyond product knowledge and superiority and focus on what's most important to the buyer."

Sales and marketing must provide reps with unique content that fuels more effective, value-focused conversations.

Value selling tools help sales reps move beyond one-size-fits-all PowerPoint decks, so they can engage today's empowered buyers. They allow reps to improve the customer experience by:

• Fine-tuning your message based on the buyer's stage in sales cycle. Buyers early in the decision-making process need to understand their challenges, so your value selling tools should quantify their pain. In the middle of the decision-making process, your tools must prove that low-risk solutions can help prospects achieve a good ROI and quick payback. This is justifying the gain. At the end of the sales cycle, your tools must prove that your solution is the best choice, or that you are not the same.

• Showing each role the unique value you can deliver to them personally, in terms they care about. It should discuss the challenges and business benefits from their perspective – not yours. For example, an operations person may be concerned about inventory turns, while a financial executive wants to know about revenue growth.

According to Ninivaggi, "The best value selling tools will provide you with flexibility in each of these situations, intelligently tuning the value messaging and quantification to match the prospect's role and stage in the sales cycle."

The best value selling tools also use the persuasion techniques discussed by both Aristotle and modern neuroscience. Ninivaggi concurs with the three required elements for sales tools:

• **Emotions.** Use stories to grab prospects' attention and make your engagements more memorable. Connecting with prospects' emotions can also help you rock the status quo and get them to take action. Your sales mix should include compelling "before-and-after" stories.

• **Logic.** Your value selling tools should go beyond sales messaging to include personalized financial quantification for each prospect. Show the costs of doing nothing, along with the ROI prospects can achieve. This will help everyone on the buying committee rationalize their decision.

• **Credibility.** Show how the prospect's peers have achieved similar savings with high return, fast payback and low risk. Relevant success stories enhance your credibility and provide third-party validation that your solution delivers results.

According to Ninivaggi, your prospects put a lot on the line when they sign your contracts. The wrong purchase decision can cost them their jobs. When you address each of these three areas, you can mitigate their personal and business risk, as well as help them build the trust they need to move forward.

Good value selling tools will also provide you with customer intelligence. If you use the tools to perform discovery – surveying and collecting information about each prospect – you will have a wealth of insights to share in future engagements. You can also use this customer intelligence to support your sales strategies, marketing content and product improvements.

ROI Sales Tools: Help Prospects Financially Justify Your Solution

Today's prospects require ROI. However, leaving it up to them to determine their ROI can lead to stalled deals and longer sales cycles.

Arm your sales reps and partners with ROI tools to help prospects understand your value and deliver a CFO-ready business case. These tools will give prospects the financial
justification they need to validate the investment's worthiness and gain approvals.

ROI sales tools make it easy to:

Take a look at ROI tools:

Windows ROI Analysis

DataCore Benefits Calculator for Software-Defined Storage

View these tools at
FrugalnomicsSurvivalGuide.com/ resources

• Show the exact business benefits that your solution provides

• Tally the investments

• Calculate ROI and other key metrics

These tools contain discovery questions that will help sales reps interact with prospects. Reps can collect information about prospects' current practices, legacy solutions and costs.

From there, ROI tools will calculate the prospect's current costs, process challenges, risks and missed revenue opportunities. Then, they configure and price a solution that will best meet the prospect's requirements. The ROI tools will also tally the total costs for planning, integrating, delivering and supporting the solution.

Next, the tools will simulate the impact of the proposed solution versus the prospect's current costs and challenges. They quantify the business benefits of your solution – including cost savings, process improvements, risk mitigation and revenue impact.

Finally, the tools provide an ROI analysis, calculating the investments versus benefits to tally a cash flow. They provide the following key financials to help prospects justify investments:

• **ROI** – a ratio of benefits versus costs

• **Payback** – how quickly the project earns benefits to overcome required investments

• **NPV savings** – a look at the net cash flow, factoring in the time-value of money and risk via a discount rate

HOW TO DIFFERENTIATE YOURSELF IN A HIGHLY COMPETITIVE MARKET

Jim Ninivaggi – Service Director, Sales Enablement Strategies, SiriusDecisions

In today's market, it's difficult to distinguish yourself on the basis of your company, product, service or price. The vendors who excel are those who not only sell better than the rest but also deliver a better customer experience.

However, most sellers miss the mark by pitching products versus selling value. They don't meet the minimum expectations of today's prospects, much less deliver a superior experience.

Delivering a better experience begins and ends with the customer conversation – the precious time sales reps spend with prospects. The key question to ask is, "Are my sales reps effectively articulating and delivering value in each conversation?"

If you can't answer "yes", you must take action.

Arm your sales reps with the right value content, conversations and quantifications.

You also must go beyond handing reps a new sales methodology book or sending them to a hot workshop. Provide value sales training and coaching, so they have the competence and credibility to effectively engage prospects.

The key is a combination of value messaging, tools, training and coaching to empower sales reps to articulate your value and provide a superior customer experience.

Jim Ninivaggi

Sales reps and prospects can use the full ROI analyses later in the sales cycle to produce a business case.

ROI sales tools can also include scope control for use earlier in the sales cycle. They can:

• Fine-tune the analysis scope to tally the prospect's "costs of doing nothing", saving the ROI and benefits tallies for later in the sales process.

• Include a diagnostic assessment to compare the prospect's current practices against the competition.

Additional keys to improving ROI sales tool success include:

• Keep the tool simple. Layer the questions and results, so you don't overwhelm your sales reps or prospects. We recommend no more than 10-15 initial discovery questions. You can ask additional questions via a pop-up later in the process.

• Use the default values for most key metrics. In the beginning, prospects may not know the answers to key values. Providing research-based defaults helps you get early estimates that you can refine over time.

• Allow prospects and sales reps to control the results. Include only the relevant parts of the analysis based on the prospect's stage in the buyer's journey.

• Don't use "black box" calculators. These calculators ask just a few questions and then spew out magical results. Prospects don't find these calculators credible. Provide drill-downs into your calculations to give prospects greater insights into their challenges and opportunities.

• Provide third-party validation of your metrics and benefit assumptions. This will enhance your credibility.

• Integrate your ROI tool into your sales workflow. Place links to the tool in your CRM system, sales playbooks and your online portals.

• Include training and coaching. This helps sales reps know where and how to apply the tool, making them more confident and credible.

Prospects don't find "black box" calculators to be credible. Drill-downs provide transparency in your calculators and build credibility for your prospects.

81

$750k

$1.5M savings

TCO Comparison Tools: Show Prospects How You Are Different

Prospects often have a hard time distinguishing how your solution compares to competitive options. Leaving this comparison to the buyer means that you won't have an opportunity to illuminate your differences and quantify your superior value.

Total cost of ownership (TCO) is the measure of not just the purchase cost of a product or service, but its total cost over its useful life cycle. For many solutions, such as data centers, the upfront costs are a mere 20%-30% of the total ownership costs.

TCO comparison tools make the tally of these costs easier, as they compare the costs of different solutions head to head. The comparison is done over time, from the initial planning phase through retirement. It uses a chart of accounts – a common accounting framework to be sure that all costs are compared apples to apples.

Comparing your solution to the legacy solution's TCO is useful earlier in the sales cycle, when you want to prove that the prospect's current state is too costly or risky. TCO sales tools are used later in the sales cycle to help win the competitive "bake-off", when prospects are comparing your TCO to your competitors. The most successful sales teams use TCO comparisons at both stages.

TCO sales tools help reps tally the total lifecycle costs of your proposed solution versus legacy or competitive solutions. This includes comparing the capital (asset investments) and operating costs (labor, maintenance contracts, facilities, etc.).

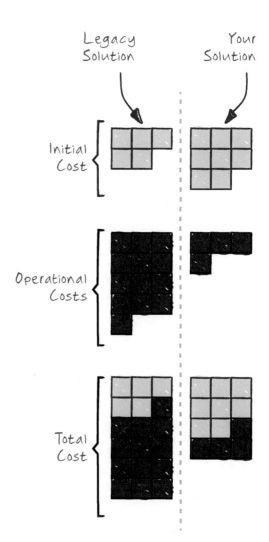

THE MYTH OF THE SINGLE SALES MODEL

Interview with Scott Santucci, former Principal Sales Enablement Analyst, Forrester Research

How is the B2B sales space changing from how it was five years ago?

There's a big myth in B2B sales and marketing. Everyone tries to say, "THE BUYER does this". However, there's no longer a single sales model, and each buyer does things differently. We now have the following four sales models:

1. **A transactional model** where buyers want to radically reduce their costs and accelerate the process of servicing customers. Buyers in this model are overwhelmed with information from vendors. In fact, they often have more information than the salespeople.

2. **An accommodative model** where a sales force already has a master service agreement with a company and wants to increase its sales. They work with strategic sourcing people – as opposed to the procurement department – to create volume discounts and customized relationships.

Buyers in this model want analytics that will help them sell more and perform better. For example, grocery store owners can use analytics on shelf space to gain insights into their inventories and sell more packaged goods.

3. **A prescriptive model where salespeople help executives solve complex problems.** Today's executives are trying to do more with less. To improve efficiencies and cut costs, many executives are integrating new technologies with their existing processes. However,

they often find the technology overwhelming and need salespeople with deep subject matter expertise to help them through this process.

4. **A performance-based model** where salespeople partner with businesses to drive results. In this model, the business has a complex problem that cuts across multiple departments. Since there are many stakeholders, the sales team must be prepared for lots of collaboration and process integration.

In this model, executives don't care about your products and services. They care about your performance. If you can help them succeed, you'll be extremely valuable. If not, you'll just be a commodity.

Today's buyers are also very uncertain. Executives are under immense pressure to grow their companies, but they fear risk (e.g. getting fired because they made the wrong decision). They may know that they need to make changes, but if you can't show how you'll reduce the risk, they won't work with you.

Do you see a gap between what most salespeople talk about and what buyers actually want to know?

Yes, the gap is huge and it's growing.

Buyers are frustrated with salespeople. This frustration is off the charts, because salespeople aren't empathetic and only talk about themselves. However, most executives don't care about your products or services. They care about how you can help them get results.

Why are sales forces so misaligned with buyers?

The biggest problem is the gap between a company's business strategy and its sales force. Many sales forces are trying to shift to a value-selling model. However, the supply chains behind these sales forces use a product-selling model. So, companies give reps the wrong training. They spend 90% of their time teaching reps about products, when prospects want to talk about results.

In addition, salespeople don't have tools that demonstrate their value. They need tools that frame the prospect's challenges and clearly articulate how they can help.

You can have the best salespeople in the world, but if they have the wrong support infrastructure or are measured against the wrong criteria, it will be difficult for them to succeed.

How can sales forces empower their teams to better engage customers?

Most vendors don't know basic things like what problem their solution solves or which stakeholders have a say in the purchase decision. The first thing you should do is **model your customers**, so you'll gain insights into their challenges and buying processes.

Then, **map your capabilities to your customer models.** Determine if you have the following:

• Content – the culmination of all the messages your salespeople must communicate

• Tools - the client-facing ways to manifest the content

• Skills – the skills your salespeople need to interact with customers

Your content, tools and skills must align with the following measurable sales objectives:

• Gaining access to buyers

• Having successful meetings with buyers

• Creating a shared vision of success with buyers

• Building a business case for a specific buyer

Finally, **match your salespeople, content and tools to your customer models.** This will help your reps deliver the greatest value – regardless of which buyer type you are working with.

Scott Santucci

Take a look at a TCO
Calculator:

**Avaya IP Office TCO
Calculator**

View this tool at
**FrugalnomicsSurvivalGuide.com/
resources**

TCO sales tools make comparisons consistent, credible and easy. They typically include:

1. A configuration questionnaire specifying which solutions to compare and configure.

2. A comparison database with up-to-date pricing and ownership cost metrics for each solution configuration and component.

3. An analysis to visualize the TCO comparison results.

The most successful TCO comparison tools also include:

1. Flexible comparisons with the ability to select and configure different solutions and select various comparison timeframes.

2. Simplicity, distilling the chart of accounts and financial analysis so as not to overwhelm the user with details, such as pricing every element and line item of each solution.

3. Third-party metrics. When customers are comparing vendors head to head, they need validation that the comparison metrics are credible, especially third-party research and certification.

As with the ROI sales tools, the TCO comparison tools should integrate with your current sales workflow. Provide access to these tools via your CRM, sales playbooks and online portals.

It's also important to train and coach your sales team on how to use these tools, as TCO can be very technical. This will help reps know where and how to apply the tool. It will also make them confident when they configure the analysis and present comparison results.

Realized Value Tools: Prove Your Ongoing Business Value

ROI is not just for pre-sales. It's also becoming important post-sale, as more business leaders demand accountability. Plus, since more solutions are sold as renewable services, they must be justified on a continuous basis.

To prove tangible business value on an ongoing basis, many organizations are implementing realized ROI solutions.

The realized ROI is used to discover and analyze a solution's benefits post-deployment. It compares key "before-and-after" metrics, tallying the cost savings, process improvements, risk mitigation and revenue benefits.

The realized ROI analysis is best used at least three months prior to renewal. You can also make it part of your value assessment program to review and analyze your realized value on a quarterly basis. A regular analysis program is preferable to waiting until just before renewal, so success can be measured and, if below expectations, managed to success.

Value Storytelling and Financial Justification: helping you connect with Prospects via Logic, Emotion and Trust

Traditional ROI sales tools and TCO comparisons are good for rational justification. However, they don't include all of the elements that are important in driving decisions. For example, they don't help prospects connect emotionally to your message via visuals or boost your credibility via success stories.

Look for tools that combine storytelling and evidence with financial justification – leveraging each element of Aristotle's art of persuasion and the neuroscience of buying – emotion, logic and evidence. These conversation tools can be used earlier in the sales cycle to tell your story and quantify your value.

One such tool is ValueStory, which presents simple discovery questions and assessments. It then assembles the right visual storytelling, financial justification and success stories – based on the discovery – helping to guide your value conversation and upfront quantification.

Visit I Want My ROI to see examples of these ValueStory-powered tools in action.

3RD PARTY CERTIFICATION IS A REQUIREMENT

Bill Kirwin, Founder of the International Institute of IT Economics

Trust, but verify is a form of advice, recommending that while a source of information might be considered reliable, one should perform additional research to verify that such information is accurate, or trustworthy. The original Russian proverb is a short rhyme that states, **Доверяй, но проверяй** (doveryai, no proveryai).

This nugget of advice was popularized in the Reagan era at the apex of the cold war with Russia. I think it exemplifies the current relationship of buyers and sellers in the Age of Frugalnomics. Indeed, there is a certain atmosphere of mutually assured destruction (MAD) when a buyer who wants and needs a product and a seller the provides a product face off at the negotiating table.

What are the conditions that precipitated these tense negotiations?

The fundamental driver of these stand offs has been the challenge of articulating the value of the proposed solution.

Why is this different today than it was 5, 10, or 20 years ago? Certainly the relationship between the buyer and seller has been by new requirements to provide tight, verifiable business cases. Also, in many cases,

there is a greater distance between the buyer and the decision maker. Where once an IT decision could be made by IT management, now the final decision lies with the other stakeholders like the CFO and / or business line management. Today deals require more than one handshake. This means that the business case is subject to greater scrutiny and higher hurdles.

In the technology universe, rapid change has been an accelerator. As the IT market has moved from silo-defined to cross discipline solutions and asset based procurement to integrated service based sourcing the complexity of analyzing the TCO and ROI of a proposal has become much more complex. Most buyers (about 70 percent) lack the resources to perform these analyses and therefore ask the seller to provide the business case which often includes a 3-5 year projection of initial costs, ongoing costs, accrued benefits both qualitative and quantitative. The sellers are happy to perform this service. After all, this is akin to asking the fox to design the henhouse. This approach breaks down when the buyer challenges the projections of the business case, drills down on the numbers, the assumptions the methodology and the logic of the seller. When the seller cannot provide validation of these elements so that the buyer can confidently run it up the decision chain, the buying cycle stalls. This is why almost sixty percent of a sales pipeline consists of stalled deals, many of which will go to a do nothing decision.

How can this risk of this be mitigated?

It has been shown that business cases that are validated by an objective third party have a much higher credibility and chance for success. There are three ways that this can be accomplished.

First is to have the specific business case reviewed by a trusted advisor. However, this is an expensive consulting engagement only applicable to very large deals.

Another approach is to have the business case development tools (i.e., TCO and ROI calculators) developed by a trusted third party. The developer should have a defensible methodology, data sources, logic and produce market checked results. A model that produces 5,000 percent ROI and a payback of 17 days is sure to be challenged, no matter who developed it! However, a good tools developer can definitely help assure credibility.

However, in most cases the seller has not turned to a 3rd party, instead developing their own tools internally, having product managers or sales engineers develop the spreadsheets used by the field to build the business cases. This is true of vendors large and small. The solution here is to make sure that an objective third party has validated these internally developed tools, and puts their "3rd party certified" stamp of approval on it.

Trust, but verify is very good advice in a world where the vendors are building the business cases and the market is driven by Frugalnomics.

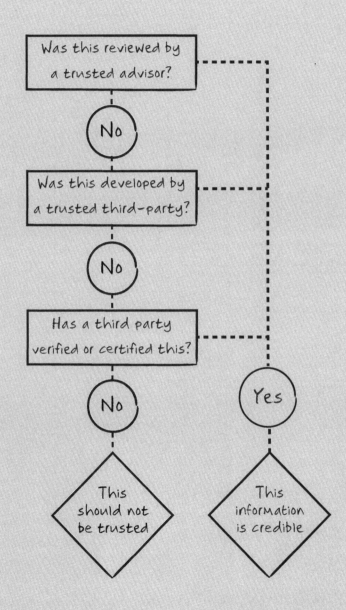

Training and Coaching Your Team to Selling Success

88% of world-class organizations have highly-qualified coaching and management teams (MHI Global)

Many sales leaders make the mistake of giving reps a new methodology or sales tool and letting them loose with very little training or guidance. However, if a salesperson isn't 100% confident with a new methodology or tool, they may not use it with a buyer. This is because their biggest fear is looking stupid in front of a prospect.

If the sales rep isn't performing, the sales leader may step in to close the deal. Not only is this poor use of the leader's time, but it also doesn't help the sales rep improve.

The best way to help sales reps overcome their fears is by practicing with them and giving them feedback in a safe environment. When you coach sales reps, you will help them gain the competencies they need to close sales.

For example, a golfer who wants to improve his game will work with a pro to learn the mechanics of a good swing. However, this methodology alone may not be enough to change his game. He needs the right tools (clubs) along with the right coaching (a caddie or coach) to really improve.

This combination of the right sales tools and the right coaching is also missing in many sales initiatives. You can't just send a golfer – or a sales rep – out without the right tools or coaching. Yet, this is what many organizations do and expect amazing sales results.

According to MHI Global, 88% of world-class sales organizations have management teams that are highly accountable for their sales teams' continuous improvement.

Here are some key components you need as part of your value selling training:

• Value selling tools that give sales reps the content, conversation points and quantification they need to succeed.

• A certification program to ensure sales reps are competent with your value messaging and tools.

• Workshops to teach sales reps about provocative prospecting, value communication and quantification.

• Motivation and justification as to why value selling is important.

• Ongoing support, so sales reps have real-time access to the latest best practices and content.

• Social community where sales reps can learn from their peers.

Good value sales training – along with an active coaching community and practice – can help reps gain competence, confidence and credibility.

If you would like to become part of an active sales community on value marketing and selling, join the LinkedIn Value Marketing and Selling group. This group is dedicated to sharing the best messaging, tools and training to help you advance from product-led selling to value selling. It features discussions on value messaging, challenger selling, proving your ROI, TCO tools and other sales best practices.

The biggest fear for any sales person is looking stupid in front of a prospect.

If reps aren't confident using a new sales tool or methodology, they won't use it out of fear of failure.

So, how do you help reps overcome these fears?

Practice with them and give them feedback in a safe environment. You can also provide them with support, so they have real-time access to the latest practices, content and advice on how to be successful.

Good value sales training, an active coaching community and practice can help reps gain competence, confidence and credibility. Value selling tools can guide them to the content, conversations and quantifications they need to succeed.

Jim Ninivaggi
Service Director, Sales Enablement Strategies, SiriusDecisions

OVERCOMING THE INSIGHTS CHALLENGE: DIAMONDS IN YOUR OWN BACKYARD

Mark Schlueter, VP Value Consultant, Alinean

Mark Schlueter

In 1913, Russell Conwell, the founder of Temple University, gave a speech called "Acres of Diamonds". The idea of "Acres of Diamonds" is that one need not look elsewhere for opportunity or fortune – the resources to achieve are present in one's own community.

Conwell told a story of a man who wanted to find diamonds so badly that he sold his property and went off in futile search for them. The new owner of his home discovered that a rich diamond mine was located right on the property. Conwell's advice is to "dig in your own backyard."

This story also applies to sales insights.

One of the biggest obstacles in implementing provocative selling is that the approach requires insights, but these insights are often difficult to gather and use.

However, your sales team can find these insights in your own backyard with the help of value selling tools.

The new breed of value selling tools automatically prompts for and collects insights from each sales conversation. The tools then aggregate these insights and apply benchmarks to future sales conversations using:

• Interactive surveys

• Diagnostic assessments

• Investment mix assessments

• Cost calculators

• Benefit calculators

These interactive tools provide insights that prospects can't find elsewhere - helping you stand out as consultative and valuable.

Sales reps and channel partners can access these tools via any device to automatically collect, create and share valuable insights from the frontline. These insights might include:

• What are prospects' priority issues and business drivers for considering a change?

• What are prospects' current capabilities and maturities, particularly the areas where they need the most help?

• What are prospects spending on solutions today?

• What is it costing them to do nothing?

• What is the estimated value they could derive if they change what they're doing?

• What are the risks and objections that prospects have in moving forward?

These answers can create valuable insights if you effectively collect, aggregate and share them.

You can challenge prospects to think differently about their business by showing them how peers – in their same role and industry – think about key issues. You can also show them how their peers are performing – with real benchmarks.

Prospects will listen if your rep shares evidence that a high percentage of their peers have similar problems. You rep can draw them into the conversation with benchmarks that compare their issues and priorities with their peers. Reps can also assess prospects' current capabilities against their peers to show if they are leaping ahead or falling behind.

Value selling tools not only help reps sell more but also give prospects "acres of insights" into their businesses.

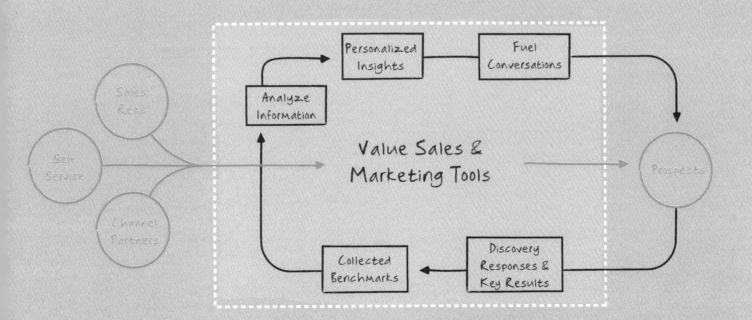

Value Management Office: Pulling It All Together

As you build you value marketing and selling program, you can tie it all together with a value management office (VMO). This office plans, coordinates, promotes and supports value marketing and selling within an organization. The VMO is responsible for:

1. Standardizing best practices for program and tools development.

2. Standardizing third-party research and tool certification.

3. Promoting awareness in the marketing/selling tools and programs.

4. Developing sales rep and channel partner education and certification programs to drive field credibility. This also creates a community for collaboration and helps you answer reps' questions.

5. Providing value consultants to assist in the largest deals and develop advanced/customized business cases.

6. Measuring and supporting adoption and success.

7. Evaluating tools on a regular basis to be sure their content and analyses remain current.

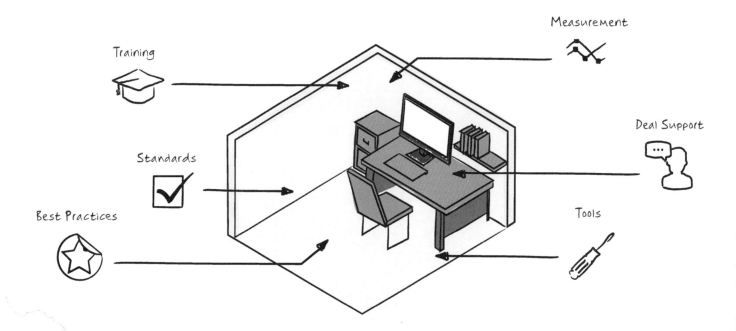

DRIVE MORE REVENUE BY BOOSTING SALES ENABLEMENT MATURITY?

Craig Nelson – Founder of SalesEnablement.com and serial sales enablement entrepreneur

Most organizations are investing more each year to train, arm and support their sales reps, but are getting less in return.

It can cost upwards of $130k each year to support a single sales rep (Forrester). And if you hire a bunch of new reps that take a long time to ramp up, or have existing reps that are not making quota and are less than productive selling new products, the ROI on Sales could be dangerously low.

"Random acts of sales enablement" are often to blame - not fully coordinating the sales training, coaching, content and tools to best effect.

To drive improvements requires the sales enablement leadership to understand their current maturity, and to drive continued improvement across all capabilities.

To help uncover and quantify your own organizations current challenges, we worked with Alinean to provide a maturity assessment and planning framework and an interactive self-assessment tool to help you synchronize your sales enablement capabilities and investments.

You can access this resource free at:

http://iwantmyroi.com/#salesEnablement-menu

Craig Nelson

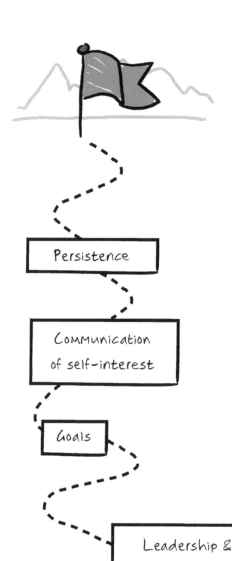

Is It Difficult to Transition from Product-Led to Value Selling?

Big rewards don't come easy.

The reality is that you must make the value marketing and selling transition to succeed. This requires time, effort and patience. Ninivaggi estimates that a successful transition can take **6—12 months**.

However, value selling's rewards far outweigh its initial efforts. In fact, value selling is likely the single greatest opportunity that your organization has. We've estimated that an average company with $100 million in sales revenue has an **additional $150 million** in Value Gap revenue opportunities at stake.

A successful transition includes:

1. Leadership and vision at the top with clear executive sponsorship and involvement.

2. Short-term goals that promote quick wins.

3. Communicating what's in it for each sales rep.

4. Being persistent, as this change will take time.

The good news? Those who have bridged the Value Gap successfully (e.g. sales enablement teams, sales reps and product marketers) know they are better than their competitors.

SURVIVAL TIPS

1

Create a Value Matrix that marketers and sales reps can use to deliver the right CLOSE messaging for any sales situation.

2

Bring the Value Matrix to life in interactive tools to help visually convey the story, deliver personalized insights and financial justification.

3

Improve your reps' selling skills by using these new methods with customers.

4

Include coaching and community to further improve customer conversations.

5

Find more tools and examples at www.alinean.com/benefits

ShoreTel Adopts Value-Led Selling and Boosts Win Rates by 28%

We've developed a reputation for proving - time after time - that we have profound economic advantages. This has shortened our sales cycles, as large customers now give us the benefit of the doubt.

Mark Arman,
Former Vice President of
Business Development,
ShoreTel

The Challenge: Gain Market Share During and After the Recession

The unified communications (UC) market is extremely competitive, with large providers battling with emerging leaders for market share. One of these emerging leaders is ShoreTel, offering brilliantly simple IP phone systems and UC solutions.

ShoreTel was growing at a rate of 50% year over year until the recession hit in 2008. During that time, the industry contracted by 15% and there was a 30% global drop in the purchase of new telecommunications equipment.

As the recession ended, ShoreTel saw a fundamental change in the telecommunications buying process. The CIO and director of telephony no longer had buying power. Instead, CIOs, CEOs and boards made the purchase decisions. In addition, more than 50% of customers required quantifiable proof that they were making the right decision when they invested in telecommunications equipment.

"ShoreTel was a challenger brand, so buyers were biased towards the market leader ," said Mark Arman, former vice president of business development at ShoreTel. "Since most of our prospects had worked with the market leader in the past, they thought it was less risky to maintain the status quo."

ShoreTel saw a big opportunity to gain market share. Many buyers didn't realize that the market leader would cost twice as much as ShoreTel over the first seven years. ShoreTel had economic advantages in terms of reliability, downtime, electricity consumption and maintenance costs.

The Losses

However, ShoreTel couldn't prove these advantages.

ShoreTel needed to tell its total cost of ownership (TCO) story. This would empower advocates to build a case for ShoreTel during board meetings. It would also disarm buyers who were biased towards the market leader.

The Opportunity: Make It Easy for Customers to Build a Business Case for ShoreTel

ShoreTel wanted to provide its sales reps and customers with a tool that would build out financial projections and show long-term TCO. This tool needed to do the following:

1. Adjust for each customer's exact circumstances

2. Base its cost estimates on independent third-party data

3. Allow customers to modify their financial assumptions

"We wanted to give customers a tool that would produce clear TCO reports," said Arman. "Then, they could take these reports to their boards and build a business case around ShoreTel's favorable TCO."

The Solution: Launch an Online TCO Tool That Quantifies ShoreTel's Value

ShoreTel launched the ShoreTel Online TCO tool, which has a public version on the company's website and a private version for partners and sales professionals. The tool analyzes the lifetime TCO of various UC solutions, comparing ShoreTel head to head with legacy phone systems and competing vendors.

Customers can log into the public tool at any time and change their assumptions. They can customize the tool for their unique architecture and location. For example, customers can get financial projections in their currencies and plug in local labor rates. When they are done, they can press a button to receive a board-ready Word report, an executive summary or a PowerPoint presentation.

"The TCO tool allowed customers to zero the price for the market leader's equipment. Customers realized that even if they didn't pay for our competitor's equipment, they would still save 30%-40% with

"ShoreTel was a challenger brand, so buyers were biased towards the market leader ... they thought it was less risky to maintain the status quo."

ShoreTel," said Arman. "This showed buyers that they should think of TCO, as opposed to basing their decision solely on upfront costs."

The TCO tool also showed customers the costs of doing nothing, which helped ShoreTel engage buyers earlier in the sales process.

ShoreTel supported its economic messaging with a Lowest TCO Guarantee program. If the TCO tool or independent third-party data proved that another vendor cost less, than ShoreTel would lower its price to beat the competition. After five years, only one customer inquired about the guarantee.

"We built the TCO story into all of our sales and marketing, as it's one of the most important proof points in this evolving and changing industry," said Arman. "Our architecture had lots of advantages, and the tool was the final proof point for these advantages."

Sales training was also a vital part of the TCO tool's success. ShoreTel certified sales reps and partners on how to use the tool. They received training via webinars, videos and in-person sessions. ShoreTel also told reps not to give customers discounts if they didn't first use the TCO tool.

By using the TCO tool and methodology, ShoreTel improved their win rate from 62% to 90%

The Evidence: Vale Selling New Sales Methods Helped ShoreTel Boost Its Incremental Revenue by More Than $301.2 Million Per Year During in the First Five Years

During a five-year ramp up, 30% of ShoreTel's on-premise solution deals involved the TCO tool and methodology. The TCO tool consistently demonstrated that ShoreTel cost 50% less than the market leader and 20%-30% less than its other competitors. This – combined with the TCO Guarantee – significantly boosted ShoreTel's competitive win rate and resulted in at least more than $30 million per year in incremental revenue over the next five years. ShoreTel's revenue was 10% higher than it would have been without the TCO tool and methodology over the first 12 months.

Since ShoreTel was able to demonstrate its economic value, it was one of the only companies in its industry to grow during the global financial crisis. While the rest of the industry was declining at a rate of 7% year-over-year, ShoreTel had zero decline in its average selling price.

Before value selling, Without the TCO tool, ShoreTel had an 's average win rate of was 62%. When sales reps used the TCO tool and methodology, win rates jumped to 90%.

"The TCO tool also helped us achieve growth after the recession, especially in major accounts," said Arman. "However, small customers also wanted to know the economic outcomes. By the time I left ShoreTel in 2012, we had closed more than several thousand customers with the new selling methods."

At the time Arman left ShoreTel, more than 250 sales reps and partners were using the TCO tool. It received more than 600 unique visitors and 150 customized reports per month.

The TCO tool also helped ShoreTel increase its margins. Customers saw how ShoreTel would benefit them over the long term and stopped focusing solely on price. With the tool, many reps closed deals at more than half a million dollars over the market leader's price.

"We've developed a reputation for proving – time after time – that we have profound economic advantages. This has shortened our sales cycles, as large customers now give us the benefit of the doubt," said Arman. "I once walked a client through the TCO tool. After 30 minutes, he said that he had all the information he needed and signed a PO the next day."

While Arman was with ShoreTel, he was brought in to help close 70 deals. He used the TCO tool to close 66. "The only four that we lost were ones where our competitor gave away equipment for free," said Arman.

A huge key to ShoreTel's success is its commitment to helping customers achieve specific outcomes. Reps always discuss outcomes and follow up to ensure that customers are hitting their targets.

"You can't be successful in solution selling if you're not personally invested in outcomes," said Arman. "This helps customers see you as a trusted advisor, which drives long-term value for both you and your customers."

Results of the Solution

- Helped drive 30% of deals
- $30M in revenue impact annually
- Maintained average selling price
- Improved win rates to 90%

CHAPTER 5

Evidence

How to Measure the Success of Your Value Marketing and Selling Programs

It's becoming more important than ever to show results on marketing campaign spending and sales enablement programs.

At Gartner our common mantra was, "you can't manage what you don't measure."

The good news is that research from IDC indicates that spending on value marketing and selling programs can return **$8.10 for every dollar invested.**

So how can you measure the success of your own value-led sales and marketing?

Measuring Value Marketing Effectiveness

Value marketing allows you to break through the noise, so you can:

• Engage more prospects

• Connect with key decision makers earlier to accelerate your sales cycles

• Improve your nurturing and facilitate buyer decisions

According to IDC, value marketing programs generate **20% more leads** than traditional campaigns. They also achieve at least a **5% better conversion rate** than traditional marketing campaigns.

To determine your value selling and productivity success, we recommend taking the following measurements:

- [x] Percentage of deals stalled in the pipeline

- [x] Percentage of deals lost to the competition

- [x] Number of months to close (i.e. average length of your sales cycle)

- [x] Average deal size to determine how much discounting and upselling is taking place

- [x] Renewal rates

- [x] Quota performance

- [x] New hire ramp-up time (i.e. the time it takes a new sales rep to perform at the same level as a veteran rep, especially the time it takes to achieve 80% or more of quota)

- [x] Improvement in selling time (i.e. reduction in the time spent on overhead tasks and increase in time spent on customer calls and conversations)

To determine if your value marketing programs are bringing you these results, take the following measurements:

1. Number of leads per month

2. Number of opportunities generated from these leads

3. Number of closed deals from these leads

You can calculate the ROI of your value marketing program with the following equation: Number of closed deals from generated leads X average deal size.

Measuring Value Selling Effectiveness

Value selling gives your reps the right messaging, tools and training – so they can hit their quotas and improve sales performance. It also allows you to quickly ramp up new hires and reduce your overhead.

When it comes to your prospects, value selling helps you:

- Engage with buyers earlier in their purchase decision

- Have more effective sales conversations

- Motivate buyers to say "yes" to each step in your sales process

- Gain faster consensus and approvals from prospects

SURVIVAL TIPS

1

Establish a measurement system to track improvements in your sales and marketing effectiveness.

2

Determine if your value marketing campaigns have impacted your number of leads per campaign and the quality of those leads.

3

Measure if your value selling program has had a positive impact on selling effectiveness. This includes your ability to get earlier meetings, reduce stalled deals, accelerate sales cycles, increase deal size, improve quota performance, reduce new hire ramp-up time, increase renewal rates and get more competitive wins.

4

Measure sales productivity improvements in reducing the time to customize presentations, recreate collateral and develop business cases.

5

Quantify the value of your improvements with the Sales Effectiveness and Marketing Effectiveness calculators in the I Want My ROI portal.

SUCCESS STORY

Adaptive Insights Empowers Field Reps with Value Selling Tools and Gets More Prospects to Say "Yes!"

> "The value selling tool helps our sales cycle move quickly... the more reps who use it, the more wins we get. The tool has helped us move more customers from doing nothing to saying 'yes' to our solution."

Paul Turner
Vice President, Product Marketing,
Adaptive Insights

The Challenge: Create a Holistic Business Case that Shows Adaptive's Economic Value

Adaptive Insights is the worldwide leader in cloud corporate performance management (CPM) and business intelligence (BI). The company's sales messaging focused on how it could help prospects plan and budget faster.

However, Adaptive's field reps were failing when they asked prospects to take the next step. Since prospects couldn't see Adaptive's economic benefits, they weren't moving forward. This lengthened Adaptive's sales cycles and impacted its revenue.

"We were talking about speeding stuff up, but we couldn't show prospects the economic benefits of our solution," said Paul Turner, Vice President of Product Marketing at Adaptive Insights. "We needed to talk about our real economic value, so we could move prospects from doing nothing to making a decision."

Adaptive wanted to show prospects its value in four key areas:

1. Acceleration

2. Cost benefits around greater productivity and fewer indirect costs

3. TCO improvements over the tools customers are currently using

4. Strategic benefits, such as growing revenue and cutting costs

"We wanted to bring these four elements into a holistic business case that would elevate the value of our solution beyond the intangibles of running your processes faster," said Turner.

The Opportunity: Empower Field Reps to be More Consultative

Adaptive wanted to empower its field reps to be more consultative. To do this, Adaptive needed a sales tool that would help reps demonstrate its value to prospects.

"We didn't want to use spreadsheets, as they are hard to maintain and don't measure engagement," said Turner.

The value selling tool had to be easy to use, so reps could quickly create business cases that would make them look credible in front of prospects. The tool also needed to measure prospect and field rep engagement.

The Solution: Provide Field Reps with a Value Selling Tool

Prior to joining Adaptive, Turner had implemented value selling programs with leading cloud ERP and HCM providers. With the ERP provider, Turner had looked at some ROI vendors, but their one-off tools were hard to maintain. He selected a vendor that had a more thoughtful and complete business case.

"Look for a vendor who can help you understand how to build a business case," said Turner. "Our vendor provided us with lots of best practices and advice on how to frame our benefits."

Turner also contacted this vendor to build Adaptive's value selling tool. It took three months to build the tool and roll it out to Adaptive's field reps.

"The key was to get feedback from the field," said Turner. "We included sales stakeholders in our calls to make sure that what we were building aligned with their needs."

The Evidence: Adaptive's Field Reps Create Compelling Business Cases and Get More Wins

Prior to launching its value selling tools, Adaptive received ongoing requests for business cases from field reps. Now, the requests have stopped. Field reps have all the information they need to create compelling business cases. They can also answer prospects' questions about ROI.

"The value selling tool helps our sales cycle move quickly," said Turner. "Field reps can instantly create business cases, answer questions and then move on to the next step. The tool also makes us look more consultative than our competition."

Adaptive also tracks the tool's online usage to help measure its success. Turner makes sure that online usage isn't dropping off and that field reps are using the tool to close sales every month.

"Field satisfaction is important to us," said Turner. "The more reps who use it, the more wins we get. The tool has helped us move more customers from doing nothing to saying "yes" to our solution."

Start Your Journey to B2B Sales and Marketing Success

The sales and marketing world is very different than it was just a few years ago, and you likely see the impact of Frugalnomics every time you try to connect with prospects.

You reach out, and it's tougher to get a response. So, you send out more messages ... but so does everyone else. The problem keeps growing, and it gets harder to make quotas.

You finally get a meeting and see how über-busy your prospect is. After the first meeting, the odds are high that you won't hear from the prospect for some time, if at all. Your prospect has too many other fires to put out and not enough resources.

For those few prospects who proceed, your first meeting leads to another, and another – all with more folks joining each call to review and render an opinion. And getting the committee on board is just the start of a tough negotiating process with procurement sure to extract their pound of flesh.

With Frugalnomics so firmly entrenched, why are so many businesses still using old-school sales and marketing approaches? Why are buyers still complaining that sales and marketing are pitching products versus talking about value? Even as marketers and sellers try to address this challenge, buyers still believe that the Value Gap is widening.

Perhaps the Value Gap hasn't impacted revenue in a catastrophic enough way to force the revolution. Or maybe your competition has also been slow to change, which makes closing the Value Gap less of a concern. Or perhaps such a significant change is hard and takes longer than any of us imagine.

I've asked many leaders and analysts why the Value Gap persists and is growing. The only consensus is no one knows for sure. However, we do know that if we don't put more effort in to value sales and marketing, the problem will only get worse and eventually have serious consequences. You can gain a huge competitive advantage by addressing the Value Gap now ... before your peers recognize its importance.

Hopefully, we have convinced you and your team how important it is to close the Value Gap. Refer back to the value messaging, tools and training framework in this book to improve your sales and marketing results.

Thank You

Thank you!

This book is the culmination of working with many great thought leaders, teammates and customers.

Big thanks to leading pundits Jim Ninivaggi, Scott Santucci, Randy Perry, Brian Hession, Craig Nelson and Bill Kirwin, the father of TCO, for continuing to challenge the status quo, and your valuable input and advice to guide our theories and solutions.

To the Alinean team, who have done something that isn't easy: helping create a market for value marketing / selling best practices and tools. Thanks for waking up every day with a passion to drive change, implement new ideas and assure customer success. Special thanks to Dan Sixsmith and Mark Schlueter for their contributions to our thought leadership and content for this book.

To our loyal Alinean customers, who have helped shape our ideas, practices and tools over the past decade. through tireless work to drive adoption and change, especially those that contributed key ideas and case studies: Mark Armen, Paul Turner, Patrick Flanigan, Doug May and Cheryl Buckner Grubbs.

To the team that helped produced this book and bring my words and voice to life: the new thinking and visual genius of Taylor Davenport, and the organization skills, expert editing and creative writing of content marketing expert Rachel Foster.

To my late mentor Dan Friedlander: who pushed me to think differently and challenge the status quo everyday. You are missed, but your influence clearly lives on.

And special thanks to my family: Judy, Sophia and Alaina for inspiring and motivating me every day to accomplish more and reach higher.

About the Author

Tom Pisello is a thought leader, author on sales and marketing effectiveness and a serial entrepreneur. He is well-known from his blog articles and newsletter as "the ROI Guy".

Tom is currently the CEO/Founder of Alinean, providing B2B sales and marketing leaders with messaging, tools and training to communicate and quantify value to ever more frugal prospects.

Prior to Alinean, Tom founded Interpose, a provider of total cost of ownership (TCO) measurement and analysis software tools and training. He founded Interpose in 1993 and sold it to Gartner in 1998. At Gartner, Tom served as Managing VP and was instrumental in Gartner's software becoming the industry standard for TCO and ROI assessment.

After leaving Gartner, Tom launched and developed several innovative companies including Full Armor, Connotate Technologies, DigitalOwl, OurBeginning.com and Puerta-Bella.com. During this time, he gained substantial start-up experience in IT management and security, big data and e-commerce.

Tom holds a BSc degree in electrical engineering from the State University of New York at Buffalo and a "mini-MBA" from Rollins College, FL.

Tom currently lives in Winter Park, a small college town located just north of Orlando, FL, with his wife and two teenage daughters.

You can follow Tom's latest writings on his blog: blog.alinean.com. You can also connect with him on Twitter (@tpisello) or LinkedIn.

Metrics that Matter

Content Marketing

Buyers now receive 32% more marketing campaigns compared to two years ago (SiriusDecisions)

The average person receives the equivalent of 174 newspapers every day (MHI Global Instititue)

The attention span of a typical buyer has dropped from 12 seconds in 2000 to 8 seconds today – that's less than the attention span of a goldfish (Statistic Brain)

It now takes 50% more leads to generate the same amount of revenue as it took just two years ago! (IDC)

5% YoY decline in white paper marketing effectiveness (DemandGen Report)

Buyers think that white papers should be seven pages. However, the average white paper is now more than 10 pages long (IDG)

94% of customers have disengaged with a vendor because they received irrelevant or poorly crafted emails (CEB)

Studies have found that 71% of business executives say content from companies turns them off when it seems more like a sales pitch than valuable information. However, 93% of marketers and sellers continue to tie their messaging and content directly to products and services. (CEB)

55% of marketers plan to increase spending on content (Content Marketing Institute / Marketing Profs, however, 60-70% of content currently goes unused (SiriusDecisions)

According to the study, respondents indicated mixed sentiment on the effectiveness of go-to content like videos (40% ineffective rating), white papers, case studies and research reports (42% ineffective) - (Content Marketing Institute / Marketing Profs

Most trusted content comes from Peers (84%) and Industry Analysts (65%) (IDC).

Only 13% of buyers view vendor-created content as credible (SiriusDecisions)

Buying By Committee

43% more stakeholders are involved in a typical B2B purchase decision compared to just three years ago (IDC)

5.4 stakeholders are involved in a typical B2B purchase decision (CEB)

An average of 10 people are involved in a typical enterprise purchase decision (>$500k) (IDC)

Sales Productivity

60% of sales time is spent not with customers but on overhead tasks (CSO Insights)

Now takes over 10 months to bring new sales reps up to speed so they can make quota. (CSO Insights)

In high technology and other complex B2B selling spaces, it can take up to three years to ramp up a new sales hire. (Forrester)

67% of buyers have a clear picture of the solution they want before they engage sales reps. (Sirius-Decisions)

Buyers now wait until their decision-making process is 57% complete before they invite sales reps and channel partners into the conversation (CEB)

The inability for sales reps to effectively articulate value is indicated as the #1 sales growth / performance challenge (71%). (SiriusDecisions)

Only 44% are highly confident in sales force's ability to communicate value messages to customers and prospects, compared to 88% for world-class Sales organizations. (MHI Global Institute)

According to buyers, a meager 10% of sales reps are perceived as value-focused (Forrester)

58% of buyers have indicated that they've disengaged with a solution provider that has not aligned with their challenges or articulated the solutions' unique value. (Qvidian Sales Execution Survey)

Only 17% of sales reps are advancing beyond the initial presentation and getting a second meeting (Forrester)

Only 40% of sales organizations clearly understand a customer's issues before proposing a solution. (MHI Global)

A majority of buyers (62%) indicate that your sales reps are knowledgeable about your company and products. However, Most reps receive very low grades (30%-40%) on their knowledge of the buyer's industry and preparation for questions they would ask, and Three out of four sales reps are perceived as having little to no knowledge about the buyer's specific business. (Forrester)

Most important sales execution challenges to executive management – 71% indicate increasing win rates, 59% say improving overall quota attainment. (Qvidian Sales Execution Survey)

Top reasons for not meeting quota goals – too many deals ending in no decision (42%), sales unable to effectively communicate value (41%) - (Qvidian Sales Execution Survey)

Most important near term Sales challenges – Difficulty presenting differentiation (29%), Difficulty establishing ROI (27%) - (Qvidian Sales Execution Survey)

Sales challenges increasing most in priority compared to prior year– improving value communication (11% increase) and personalizing content (10% increase) - (Qvidian Sales Execution Survey)

Importance of Financial Justification

95% of buyers require financial justification prior to purchase approval (IDC)

2/3rds of buyers don't have the time, knowledge or tools needed to make business value assessments and calculations. (IDC)

81% of buyers expect vendors to proactively provide a business case and quantify the value of proposed solutions. (IDC)

Impact of Frugalnomics

58% of a typical sales pipeline currently ends in "No Decision" (Sales Benchmark Index).

76% of deals go to companies that engage with prospects early in the sales cycle, helping to establish the buying agenda, while only 24% of deals go to companies that win the "bake-off". (Forrester)

Sales cycles are taking 24% longer than they did just two years ago (SiriusDecisions)

An average discount of 20% is needed to get a typical B2B sale to close (IDC)

Accenture found that only 59% of sales reps will achieve their quota this year, down sharply from 67% last year. (Accenture)

There are now $3 million in additional revenue opportunities available for every $1 million in quota because of Frugalnomics.

Value Marketing and Selling Benefits

Marketing Benefits

- 20% more leads
- 5% better conversion rates

Sales Benefits

- 5% less stalled deals
- 10% acceleration in your sales cycle
- 30% less discounting, along with an increase in order size
- 35% competitive win rate improvement
- 20% renewal rate improvement
- 15% faster sales rep ramp up time
- 5% sales productivity boost

(IDC)

Selected References

Chapter 1: Challenge

1. Knowledge Management Systems: The Single Source. (2014, September 1). Retrieved January 1, 2015, from http://www.millerheiman.com/Images/Infographics/MH-Infographic-Sept2014-v1.aspx/

2. Harald Weinreich, Hartmut Obendorf, Eelco Herder, and Matthias Mayer: "Not Quite the Average: An Empirical Study of Web Use," in the ACM Transactions on the Web, vol. 2, no. 1 (February 2008), article #5.

3-4. Corporate Executive Board (CEB) Sales and Marketing Conference 2014

5. Prioritizing Time Spent with Customers. (2014, February 1). Retrieved January 1, 2015, from http://www.millerheiman.com/Images/Infographics/MH-Infographic-Feb2014FINAL-(1).aspx/

6. Forrester Forum for Sales Enablement Professionals 2014

7. Sales Execution Trends 2014. (2013, December 1). Retrieved January 1, 2015, from http://www.qvidian.com/sites/default/files/resource/Sales-Execution-Trends-2014.pdf